Christian
Counseling

An Introduction

H. Newton Malony
David W. Augsburger

ABINGDON PRESS / NASHVILLE

CHRISTIAN COUNSELING
AN INTRODUCTION

This book is printed on acid-free paper.

Library of Congress Cataloging-in-Publication Data

Malony, H. Newton.
    Christian counseling : an introduction / H. Newton Malony, David W. Augsburger.
        p. cm.
    Includes index.
    ISBN-13: 978-0-687-33283-0 (pbk. : alk. paper)
    1. Pastoral counseling.   2. Counseling—Religious aspects—Christianity.   I. Augsburger,
David W.   II. Title.

BV4012.2.M275   2007
253.5—dc22

                                                                                            2006024999

07 08 09 10 11 12 13 14 15 16—10 9 8 7 6 5 4 3 2 1

MANUFACTURED IN THE UNITED STATES OF AMERICA

Contents

Introduction

THE TOPIC OF CHRISTIAN COUNSELING came up on a winter camping trip. The campers sat around a snow table they had dug out of the snow with a folding shovel. As usual, these hiking buddies of thirty years began to share their lives—the questions, doubts, tragedies, stresses, achievements, and changes that make up human existence wherever it may be found. All of them were active Christians. So, as usual on every trip, religious faith entered into the conversation.

Don asked the question: "If you were flying from Los Angeles to New York, would it matter to you whether or not the pilot was a Christian?" Almost to a person they answered, "No! It would matter that the pilot was skilled and experienced in flying airplanes, but the pilot's religious faith would be of no consequence."

Don asked another question: "If you needed a counselor, would it matter to you whether or not the counselor was a Christian?" Almost to a person they answered, "Yes!" "Why?" Don queried. The chorus of answers ranged from "I would not want my counselor to denigrate my faith" to "A Christian counselor would have a different view of health" to "I would hope my faith would help me solve my problems" to "Counseling is different from flying airplanes" to "A non-Christian counselor might not believe in God" to "I would want my counselor to pray for me" to "Counseling deals with your mind, your way of looking at life, not just carrying your body from place to place in an airplane." Their conversation went long into the night.

We might get an equally long list of answers from those who would agree that whether the counselor was Christian or not was important for reasons that were clearly different from those given by these camping companions. Some might think that "Christian counseling" was a plague to be avoided! They would definitely *not* want to mix theirs or anybody else's religion with the help they received.

This book on Christian counseling addresses both the *need* and the *problem* that this vignette points out. Some may even question whether there is a *need* for another book on the subject. After all, religious counselors have been around for years and almost all of the nation's seminaries have offered training in counseling for much of the last century. The public would probably assume that the counseling they received from the thousands of pastors trained in these seminaries would already be "Christian." Furthermore, associations such as the American Association of Pastoral Counselors (AAPC), the Christian Association for Psychological Studies (CAPS), and the American Association of Christian Counselors (AACC) publish journals and have well-established clienteles who have attended annual conventions for many decades.

The label *Christian counseling* no longer paints a picture of a back-alley endeavor engaged in by a raving sectarian. It has become mainstream. A number of authors boldly use this title in books they have published. In addition, a new Society for Christian Psychology has recently been formed. Not a few professionals have begun to list themselves in telephone books and on marquees as "Christian," and others use this label in brochures defining the scope of their services.

However, using these facts to say there is no *need* for a new book on Christian counseling would be shortsighted, in our opinion. In both the popular and scholarly world there is a new postmodern openness to explicitly religious points of view that has only timidly been acknowledged and affirmed. The American Psychological Association (APA) is but one among a number of professional groups that recently included religion among their lists of diversities to which their members must attend in offering service. The *Diagnostic and Statistical Manual of Mental Disorders DSM-IV* has now included a "V code" for possible religious issues that might become the focus of attention in treatment.[1] Although Christians in the counseling world may have to temper any presumptions they have had that their faith has absolute proven validity, they now may have the opportunity to sit at the table of counseling approaches and claim the right to speak. We are convinced there is a *need* to which this volume is addressed.

Concerning the *problem* of Christian counseling, just what is it? In spite of many adherents, we doubt there is a common agreement on the essentials, much less the details. Most important, Christian counseling has been assumed to exist when it has not, or has been simplified beyond recognition when it does exist. The problem of Christian counseling goes far beyond what methods are used or the audacious claim that the counselor is a stand-in (translate *incarnation*) for Jesus. Of course, there is the perennial problem regarding the difference between what the counselor *says* and what the counselor *does*—an issue that has plagued schools of counseling *ad infinitum*. Nevertheless, if the Christian approach wants to coexist with other counseling theories in the twenty-first century, it must come to the table with a basic metatheory and an agreed-upon set of applications.

Both of us have been trainers of counselors for many years. At Fuller Theological Seminary, where we teach, one of us has been Professor of Pastoral Counseling and the other has been Professor of Clinical Psychology. In the past, neither of us has routinely used the label *Christian counseling* to depict what we were doing. However, all our students were Christians and each of them was being trained to be a counselor. Furthermore, the Christian faith was always at the center of our thinking. Although we have intentionally shared with our students the findings of the social/behavioral sciences about the dynamics of human behavior, we have likewise always incorporated Christian biblical and theological reflection into our training. We hoped that our students would become pastors and psychologists who *integrated* their faith into their principles, their professions, and their personal lives. We perceived ourselves as training "Christians who counseled," more than "Christian counselors."

Most important, a new cultural and philosophical postmodern environment has emerged in which tradition-specific services have gained a new legitimacy. This new outlook has made a place for Christian counseling heretofore not anticipated, envisioned, or conceived. We have decided that any timidity we may have had in using the term *Christian counseling* may have been because of a modern Babylonian captivity in which we paid too much homage to current psychological theory instead of boldly proclaiming our explicit reflections on the implications of Christian faith for counseling practice.[2] The late Menninger Foundation psychologist Paul W. Pruyser voiced concern about the same possibility in his well-known volume *The Minister as Diagnostician: Personal Problems in Pastoral Perspective* (1976).

These comments lead to what we intend to do in these pages. We have no intention of doing a survey and, on the basis of the results, describing what Christian counselors do. In an unapologetic manner, we intend to detail the parameters of what we firmly believe should be the foundations and applications of Christian counseling. Although we do not deny that these foundations include procedures as well as styles, we reason that unique convictions about the nature of reality provide the essential foundation for those who would be bold enough to claim the title "Christian counselor." In the words of the maxim "There is nothing more practical than a good theory," we assert there is nothing more important for Christian counseling than a good theology. Thus, we unabashedly claim that the intent of this volume is to be prescriptive, not descriptive.

We conceive the issues under three headings: Foundations, Applications, and Destiny. This format provides a way for us to suggest in the Foundations section the essential rudiments we feel are beginning assumptions for the task of Christian counseling. In the Applications section, we discuss a number of problem areas we think will be encountered by Christian counselors. We do not intend this list to be exhaustive, just representative. Finally, in the last section, Destiny, we describe more fully the nature of the postmodern world in which Christian counselors must function. Herein we note the need for counselors to boldly explicate their unique approach but also just as boldly engage in efforts to demonstrate that Christian counseling has a positive effect in helping persons. Showing that Christian counseling is a valid treatment option will assure respect beyond any proof that its tenets are absolutely true or not.

Finally, a word about specific concerns and writing styles—each of us came to this project with a unique history. One of us has demonstrated a profound appreciation for the subtle dynamics of the human experience resulting from depth training and writing on the task of pastoral counseling. The other of us has been immersed for years in the study of the psychology of religious experience and clinical research. Readers will easily perceive these different styles of writing in the chapters that follow. We affirm the validity of each approach and present this volume as a jointly written document rather than two books under one cover. We have critiqued and rewritten each other more than once. We offer these ideas in the hope that they will provoke dialogue and reflections among many Christian counselors in the days ahead. We acknowledge that we have been part of an evangelical Christian community of scholars for several decades. Although we are fully aware that the larger umbrella under which we have labored has been Calvinistic, we sincerely hope that we have significantly influenced that environ with our Mennonite and Methodist identities.

H. Newton Malony
David W. Augsburger
Epiphany, 2006

1. For a fuller discussion of this inclusion, see H. Newton Malony, "The V62.89 Code of the DSM-IV-R: Boon and Bane for Christian Psychologists," *Theology News and Notes* 53, no. 1 (2006): 10-11, 25.

2. See J. Sharfenberg, "The Babylonian Captivity of Pastoral Care," *Journal of Pastoral Care* 8 (1954): 124-34.

Part I

Foundations

CHAPTER ONE

Christians Who Counsel

FORMER MISSIONARY PAUL HIEBERT told a hypothetical story that sets the stage for a discussion of the distinction between "Christians who counsel" and "Christian counseling." "Suppose," Hiebert said, "A man from a rural Indian village came home and said to his wife 'I've become a Christian.' And suppose his wife would exclaim, 'Oh, how so?' If the man answered, 'I learned a new song today from a man in the village square—"Jesus loves me, this I know, for the Bible tells me so." ' And the man sings the song for his wife. Would this man be a Christian?" Most folk faced with Hiebert's question would quickly answer, "No, being a Christian involves more than singing 'Jesus loves me, this I know.' "

More to the point of the present discussion, would knowing and/or being able to sing "Jesus loves me, this I know, for the Bible tells me so" be sufficient for counselors to call themselves *Christian* and to claim they were offering *Christian* counseling? In a provocative volume entitled *Christians Who Counsel*, Ray Anderson (1990, 14) describes a counselor he knows with these words:

> Being a Christian as well as a psychologist, Sue Johnson feels assured of her salvation through Christ. She would say that her life was transformed through coming to know God as Savior and Lord of her life. She would insist that she believes in the efficacy of both prayer and the Bible for her own life of faith and growth as a Christian. And

when pressed, she would say that she believes that the Bible and Christian faith are resources for emotional healing for others as well.

These words go far beyond the singing of a song. They include a number of Christian code words that call out for elaboration. They include both Christian *substance* and Christian *practice*. However, each of the ways Anderson describes Sue Johnson could be said to be affirmations that build upon the theme of "Jesus loves me, this I know, for the Bible tells me so."

We have become convinced that "Jesus loves me, this I know" is, indeed, the basic conviction underlying the personal faith of all Christian counselors and "Jesus loves you, this I know" is the foundational, the essential, the initial, and the pervasive presumption underlying all Christian counseling wherever it may be found.

The late Henri Nouwen told a beautiful story that illustrates this truth in a profound manner. While pastor of Daybreak, a residential community for mentally challenged persons in Toronto, Nouwen was asked by Janet to give her a blessing. He responded in a somewhat automatic way by tracing the sign of the cross on her forehead. "No, that doesn't work," Janet said, "I want a real blessing!" After apologizing to her, Nouwen said he would give her a *real* blessing later at the prayer service, which he did. He enveloped her with the sleeves of the long white robe he was wearing. Spontaneously, Janet put her arms around him and laid her head against his chest. As they held each other, Nouwen said, "Janet, I want you to know that you are God's Beloved Daughter. You are precious in God's eyes. Your beautiful smile, your kindness to the people in your house, and all the good things you do show us what a beautiful human being you are. I know you feel a little low these days and that there is some sadness in your heart, but I want you to remember who you are: a very special person, deeply loved by God and all the people who are here with you" (1992, 57-59).

A better underlying assumption for Christian counseling does not exist. It parallels, to some degree, nonreligious counseling theories such as client-centered therapy, where "unconditional positive regard" is seen as essential (cf. Rogers 1957). However, for Christians, the affirmation "Jesus loves you, this I know" is grounded in convictions about love that come from outside the person, that is, from God. It is not just an attitude stemming from within the counselor (cf. Malony 1983). When Christian counselors (pastoral or professional) express to those they are trying to help, "You are a very special person, deeply loved by God" (as did Henri Nouwen), they are expressing absolute convictions about the nature of the universe, not just adopting therapeutic attitudes. They see the person's worth not as something they bestow in relationship, but as something they appraise as God-given, as grounded in the way the universe works.

Benjamin Beit-Hallahmi detailed this critical distinction about the source of Christian convictions in an essay where he compared religious experience to aesthetic appreciation (1986). Artistic creation as well as worship is an expression of the human capacity to imagine—to transcend the objective reality of the five senses. But, for religionists, especially those of the Judeo-Christian persuasion, the report of the experience is more than simply an expression of the human capacity for aesthetic appreciation. Religionists report they have been in contact with Almighty God; they give substantive reality to the experience that goes significantly beyond enjoyable representation. As Beit-Hallahmi suggests, "Thus, religion can be defined as that form of art which is claimed to be not just beautiful, but also true" (p. 7). Although the "imaginative process" may be similar for art and for religion, truth for artists is *artistic truth* (or illusion), whereas for faithful believers it is *absolute truth*.

When Christians encapsulate their religious experience in such words as "For God so loved the world that he gave his only Son, that whoever believes in him should not perish but have eternal life" (John 3:16), they are expressing an absolute, not simply an artistic, truth. In fact, this is what distinguishes religion from spirituality. The two terms are often confused. They are not the same. Spirituality is the human capacity to experience transcendent reality and immanent presence. Indeed, *spirituality* may be a quasi-religious synonym for Beit-Hallahmi's *imagination*. However, when words are put to the spiritual experience, then religion appears. Religion, thus, could be defined as the "words given to the spiritual experience." The intent of these religious words is to give meaning to the experience and to assure that the spiritual experience will reoccur (Malony 1998). The words of John 3:16 illustrate how these words

5

of the Christian faith achieve this joint purpose: "For God so loved the world that he gave his only Son" (words that provide the meaning of the experience), "that whoever believes in him should not perish but have eternal life" (words that provide the rationale for repeating the spiritual experience). These words frame the experience within a conviction about ultimate reality and they provide a way to reexperience being loved by God.

Being clear about the underlying assumptions of such religious truth statements would seem critically important for those who claim to engage in Christian counseling, and it is to a discussion of these matters that we now turn. Those who mount shingles on their doors reading "Christian Counselor" should be just as informed about the nature of the label *Christian* as they are about the label *Counselor*. Simple Sunday-school repetition of religious jargon will no more suffice than will lack of training in counseling for those who attach *Christian* to the service they provide.

Christianity—A Unique Religion

The distinction we made above between "spirituality" and "religion" is important because it could be said that, whereas all persons are spiritual, not all persons are religious. Probably it is better to say that since being spiritual is a human capacity rather than an instinct or even a need, all persons are capable of being, but not all persons are, spiritual. Every person *can* experience transcendent reality and immanent presence, but not every person *does*.

Then it would follow that although everyone is able to put words to their spiritual experiences, that is, become religious, not all persons do. Many people today speak of themselves as spiritual but not religious. It is important for those who seek the help of Christian counselors to know that Christians are not just spiritual; they are also religious. Christians are among those who have put words to their spiritual experience—many words! Christian counselors represent a tradition that has put specific, unique, and distinctive words to spirituality (the experience of transcendent reality).

Although the historic creeds have described more than adequately the content of these verbal affirmations, what follows is an attempt to detail a typology that does honor to the distinctive character of the Christian faith. Clarity about these specifics is important for Christian counselors to have in mind lest they fall into the trap of communicating an amorphous conglomerate of quasi-religious ideas to those they counsel.[1] Since impulsive use of whatever treatment comes to mind (thoughtless eclecticism) is an all-too-common danger in all counseling, we should expect no less a temptation among Christian counselors.

The Christian faith, first of all, is *monotheistic* in that it affirms one God who is apart from the natural world and human beings.

Next, the Christian faith is *historical* in that it affirms that this one God has acted in time to create the universe and all life within it. God continues to act in history by directing, supporting, and encouraging human beings.

Then, the Christian faith asserts that God intends all creation to eventually fulfill a purpose God has determined for it. The life of creation does not move around in circles, getting nowhere. Life is intentional. God has a will; God intends life to go somewhere. Thus, Christianity is *teleological*.

The Christian faith is, subsequently, *revelational*. God has made known God's purpose for all of creation through inspired teachers, writers, prophets, and, especially scriptures (the Bible). Humans are not ignorant; they have been informed.

Amazingly, the Christian faith is *experiential*. Human beings are invited and encouraged to relate personally with God. God is not a distant deity who stands apart from creation. God is eager to interact and relate with persons. In fact, God has chosen to covenant with human beings in achieving God's redemptive work in the world.

The Christian faith, therefore, is *transactional* in that the purpose of God for creation is that humans join God in creating a world where people live together in mercy, in justice, in love, and in peace. Humans cannot fulfill God's purpose for their lives individually— without interacting with others. God intends that life be lived relationally.

Unfortunately, the Christian faith is *realistic* in its appraisal of whether the will of God has been actualized in creation. So far, it has not. Humans, created in the image of God, have fallen short of God's will for them. They have failed. They have sinned.

Fortunately, however, God is busy in the process of *restoring* all creation to its original purpose and *redeeming* human beings from living God-less lives.

Most important, the Christian faith is *incarnational* in that God deliberately decided to appear on earth to reveal God's purposes through Jesus of Nazareth—called the Christ, the Messiah, the Son of God. All humans need to know about God as seen through the life, the teachings, the death, and the resurrection of this one man, Jesus. God has acted in history to *reclaim* all creation through Jesus.

It follows that Christianity is *salvific* in that it provides a means, through faith, whereby persons can rededicate their lives to God's purposes; can be forgiven for their past lives; can experience freedom from their addictions; and can find consolation when they fail, courage to face stress and tragedy, and strength to rededicate themselves to God's will and way.

Among all the world's religions, the Christian faith is *communal* in that those who experience salvation from sin and commit themselves to God's way do not act alone. God has made a covenant with humans. They become part of the people of God moving across history as a body, the church. They covenant together to support one another, be open to the guidance of God's Holy Spirit, and to work together for good.

Finally, the Christian faith is *eschatalogical,* which means that in the final analysis God holds all of history within God's creative/redemptive power. At the end of time, God will achieve God's purposes for all of creation—in nature as well as in humans. Revelation 11:15 states what Christians believe, that the day will come when "the kingdom of the world has become the kingdom of our Lord and of his Christ."

This typology is not meant to be exhaustive, but it is meant to be inclusive. All Christian counselors should be intentional in the way they espouse and practice these insightful affirmations and should be clear about the theory that guides practice. This is not unlike the way that all ego psychologists, psychoanalysts, cognitive behaviorists, or client-centered counselors utilize their unique approaches in the services they provide. Christian counselors who radically depart from these foundational components of faith do so at their own peril and run the risk of distorting the Christian label they represent. Of course, no counselor reiterates the total theory that guides their service every time they interact with clients; but they hold their particular theory in their minds as a *metatheory* in all that they do.

We feel strongly that Christian counseling offers unique features over and beyond simply the provision of warmth, insight, and empathy. In fact, we remain convinced that whereas states license counselors to offer unsupervised service to the public out of the conviction they will be professional and do no harm, so Christian counselors should feel equally responsible to the Christian faith tradition they represent. By no means do we contend that the state should take over the authorization of those who would claim to do Christian counseling, but we wonder whether churches whose members claim to offer such services should not authenticate themselves in some manner. Pastoral counselors are most often clergy who have been ordained (meaning judged able to represent the gospel in word and table) by ecclesiastical bodies. Perhaps, nonclergy counselors should be similarly approved—accountable to a "watch-care" committee that meets regularly to review their work. These bodies could conceive of themselves as approving (ordaining?) Christian counselors to the role of "word and *service.*"

This chapter has considered the question, Who are Christians who counsel? We have offered some general comments about the foundation of Christian counseling being embedded in the affirmation that each person is created and loved by God. In addition, we distinguished between spirituality and religion as well as offered a typology of the Christian faith that we believe should be the basic corpus that guides counseling services that bear the label *Christian.* Left for future chapters are crucial suggestions as to how these Christian affirmations can be incorporated into the counseling provided to those whose lives are disrupted by stress, strife, success, failure, and tragedy. This will be the task of applied Christian psychotheology to which we now turn.

1. See Wesley Brun, "A Proposed Diagnostic Schema for Religious/Spiritual Concerns," *Journal of Pastoral Care and Counseling,* vol. 59 *Supplement* (no. 5):425-41, 2005, for an example of such diffusive thinking.

CHAPTER TWO

Who Wants
Christian Counseling?

M UCH IS BEING MADE these days about truth in mar-
keting. This is nothing new. People have always wanted
to examine merchandise before they bought it. Today,
however, sellers are advised to make sure folk are fully informed
lest sellers be taken to court for not disclosing what will happen
when a purchase is made. This is a day where buyers are self-
conscious about their rights. Counseling is no exception to this
rule. Counselors are in business. They have a product to sell.
They offer service that meets a human need just as surely as does
a grocer.

In the last chapter, we noted how important it was for Christian
counselors to be very familiar with the distinctives of the
Christian faith, or else they may be accused of having nothing to
offer that is any different from those counselors not using
Christian on the signs outside their offices. In this chapter we
emphasize the importance of spelling out those distinctives so that
persons will become aware of what they can expect when they
come for Christian counseling.

"Buyer beware" used to be the maxim. However, for counselors,
"seller beware" is the better rule to follow. People are very vulnerable
when they arrive for counseling. Counseling costs time and money.
Counseling is an intrusion into everyday life that no one chooses if

they can help it. Individuals' need for help is great and promises of help can easily balloon into expectations of cure. One counselor we know was sued for not fulfilling an "implied" promise to cure a client's chronic depression. Similar litigation could possibly result where counselors use superlative religious words such as "reconciliation," "salvation," "forgiveness," and "peace."

Thus, as a prologue for discussing the topic "Who Wants Christian Counseling?" we want to emphasize how important it is for counselors to be explicit and careful in what they promise those who come to them for help. We advise all counselors to have a printed brochure to give to every client. And the words in that brochure should be chosen with great deliberation. The possible negative as well as positive outcomes should be noted. All counseling involves risk. This is no less true of Christian counseling than of other types of counseling.

In one case we know well, the counselor stated in her brochure, "I utilize the theory of Transactional Analysis and the values of the Christian faith." Below this statement the counselor listed a series of activities that she might recommend from time to time. This list included "reading from the Holy Bible." After looking over the list, one new client said, "This business of reading from the Bible . . . I want you to know I am not religious." The counselor was taken aback but replied wisely, "Thank you for letting me know this. I will not impose religion upon you." At least, both the client and counselor were honest with each other. The client now knew what *not* to expect and the counselor knew what would *not* be helpful. An ironic caveat followed, however. Several weeks later this same client brought in the brochure and asked, while pointing to the item about Bible reading, "Is there something I should be reading here?"

Nonreligious Reasons

This incident about Bible reading provides a segue into considering some of the reasons people give for seeking Christian counseling. The nonreligious client who asked about Bible readings did not know beforehand that her counselor was Christian. Now it might be said that she should have known because, in this case, the counselor was on the staff of a counseling service that was clearly labeled *Christian*. Interestingly, it is not unusual for nonreligious people to seek the help of Christian counselors. Why would they do such a thing?

Maybe the Christian counseling service was located near where they lived. Maybe the Christian counseling service offered reduced-rate sessions. Maybe they chose to seek help from the first service that caught their eye in the yellow pages of the telephone directory. Maybe they heard that Christian counselors cost less than others. Contrary to these reasons, many nonreligious persons seek help from Christian counselors because those counselors have a reputation for offering helpful service. Certainly that has been our experience with the Christian counselors we have known. Most are known in their communities for being effective and compassionate—often over and beyond those who make no claim to be religious in any way.

Thus, some who come to Christian counselors may, indeed, have made that choice on the basis of reputation. Like the nonreligious client described above, they may want a Christian *counselor* but not necessarily want Christian *counseling*. However, they may have the confidence that the help they get will be of high quality. One might hope that the reputation of good counseling would be more important to nonreligious persons than announcements in the yellow pages, nearness to residence, or even the cost of the service.

We are bold enough to think that the good reputation of most Christian counselors is grounded in their personal faith that God has acted in their own lives and called them into a vocation of mercy and service. They conceive of themselves as engaged in "incarnational ministry," although in no sense do they see themselves as divine. In their counseling, they perceive that they are doing the continuing work of God as seen in Jesus, who *was* the Incarnate Word. They feel that they are engaged in a holy task whereby they have been given the opportunity to help bring in God's kingdom through the lives of those they serve. Thus, their Christian faith and *the* Christian faith lie beneath their counseling effectiveness.

The cost of counseling should not be dismissed, however. Most people expect counseling to be cheaper behind those marquees labeled *Christian*. This could be because Christian counseling is often confused with pastoral counseling—that form of help offered by parish clergy. Usually, parish clergy do not charge for their services. This perception about pastoral counseling is not exactly correct, however, because most clergy are actually paid for the counseling they offer through the salaries they receive and from the offerings of their congregations. Counseling is part of their job. They offer service but do not usually accept "fee for service." To charge extra for counseling would be considered simony—a practice discouraged by most denominations. Nevertheless, the expectation that one will not have to pay for the time clergy spend on counseling is sometimes extended to Christian counselors.

However, as often as not, Christian counselors are nonclergy. They are rarely salaried employees on church staffs. They offer fee-for-service counseling in the same manner that lawyers bill for time they spend in consultation. Christian counselors have to eat! They shop at the same grocery stores as everybody else. They drive the same cars, make the same house payments, and wear the same clothes. Nonetheless, it is a fact that people often expect Christian counselors to cost less than their nonreligious counterparts.

What are Christian counselors to do? Our conviction is that Christian counseling should be entered into with the awareness that the Christian faith is more than a profitable niche in the marketplace. By its nature, Christian counseling is part of God's witness to the world. Although Christian counselors should seek appropriate recompense for their service, they should also hold an equal concern for the welfare of those who seek their help as for themselves. They may follow the example of Paul's tent-making ministry and be content with a minimalist approach to life.[1] This does not mean they should not charge for their counseling. It does mean that they, like all licensed counselors, should offer some pro bono counseling as well as not turn away persons for lack of ability to pay. Yet they should not deny to themselves their need to survive and care for their families. Balancing these needs against the expectation that they will offer counseling for less cost is a continuing struggle that should be acknowledged and embraced by those who claim to be Christian counselors.

Religious Reasons

We turn next to religious reasons given for seeking the help of Christian counselors. Some persons report they do not want their faith challenged or discounted by nonbelievers. They have heard horror stories about counselors who think that religion is part of what made them sick or caused their problems. According to these stories, counselors who are not Christian think that religion is for the weak-minded and they will advise persons to give up their faith. By going to a Christian counselor, persons think they can be sure this will not happen.

Actually, this reason for choosing to seek the help of a Christian counselor has some truth to it. It is well known that modern counseling practice owes much to Sigmund Freud, who called himself an atheist. Freud was convinced that religion was a sign of neurotic regression rather than an aspect of good mental health. Many counselors from Freud's time to the present have bought into this thesis. Albert Ellis (1956), a proponent of Rational Emotive Therapy, was an outspoken advocate of these ideas in the last half of the twentieth century. He concluded that religious faith was bad for one's mental health because it encouraged guilt as well as incited preoccupation with God's will rather than self-interest. Ellis, as well as some other modern counselors, would recommend that a client's religion be among the first parts of life to be given up in efforts to recover from emotional disturbance.

Many persons do not agree with Ellis. Seeking help from those counselors who call themselves Christian assures them that they will still have their faith when counseling is over. Now, their concern takes two forms. One form could be a desire to have a Christian *counselor,* but not Christian *counseling.* The other form could be a desire to have Christian *counseling* as well as a Christian *counselor.* *Counselor* has to do more with the person of the counselor—whether she or he is a Christian or not; whether she or he thinks religious faith is a good thing or not. *Counseling* has to do more with the techniques the counselor uses—whether or not counselors bring religion into their treatment insights and recommendations.

Actually there are variations in these two forms that result in a fourfold model for understanding whether clients will want a Christian counselor and/or Christian counseling. The model below illustrates these:

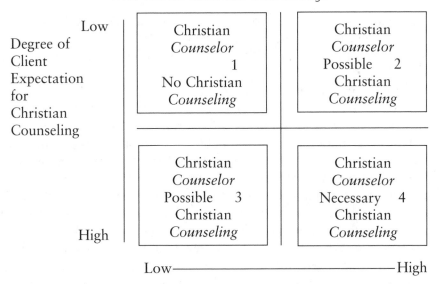

	Low——————————————High

Low

Degree of
Client
Expectation
for
Christian
Counseling

High

Christian
Counselor
1
No Christian
Counseling

Christian
Counselor
Possible   2
Christian
Counseling

Christian
Counselor
Possible   3
Christian
Counseling

Christian
Counselor
Necessary   4
Christian
Counseling

Low————————————————High

Counselor Expectation for Christian Counseling

In Quadrant 1—Christian counseling is not expected and is not necessary.

In Quadrant 2—Christian counseling is not expected but would probably occur.

In Quadrant 3—Christian counseling is expected but is only possible.

In Quadrant 4—Christian counseling is expected and is essential.

At first glance, two of these forms appear identical. Both include "Christian Counselor: Possible Christian Counseling." The only difference between the two is the level of expectation concerning whether the counseling itself will be *Christian* or not on the part of the client, as opposed to the counselor. In Quadrant 2, the inclusion of Christian *Counseling* happens as a surprise to the client, but the counselor would intend it to happen. Christian counseling would not be resisted. In Quadrant 3, the inclusion of Christian *Counseling* is expected by the client but would not be considered absolutely necessary by the counselor.

An example might help to make this difference clearer. Suppose a client sought help with a marriage problem from a Christian counselor. The reason he chose this counselor was because the counselor's office was near where he worked. The counselor, in turn, explained in the first session that he utilized a Christian framework in helping resolve marriage problems. The client acquiesced without fully realizing what this meant. This is Quadrant 2.

However, if another person sought help with a marriage problem from a well-known counselor because that individual advertised in the yellow pages of the telephone book that she was a Christian counselor, he might anticipate the counselor would explicitly use overt Christian resources; but the counselor might not be as strongly committed to this approach. This is Quadrant 3.

Quadrant 1 is where it is expected that the counselor will be Christian but where the client does not expect—and might even resist—Christian reasoning being brought into the treatment. Here, two expectations may be operating. These clients may want the security of knowing their counselors share their faith but they may expect their counselors to employ the best modern psychotherapeutic procedures available and not mix religion into the treatment. They would not think their religion had much to do with either causing or alleviating their problems. They might even feel that if they wanted Christian counseling they would have gone to their pastors for help. Yet, knowing that their counselors will not discount or challenge their faith is of prime importance for these individuals.

Quadrant 4 is where persons expect their counselors to be Christian and where they would be disappointed if their counselors did not include Christian ideas in the treatment they rendered. The kind of Christian reasoning that might be expected could be of two basic kinds: confrontive and encouraging. In *confrontive* Christian counseling, counselors might point out ways in which the difficulties being faced could be because of the ways in which persons were behaving that were out of step with Christian understandings of right and wrong, good and bad, sinful and faithful. Here the presumption might be that God has a will for life that if violated will result in disruption and confusion. The implied promise in confrontation is that resolution of problems and restoration of relationships can occur if persons change their behavior or way of looking at life. For example, if a young adult Christian sought help with depression over having flunked a college course, the counselor might point out that continuing to be self-punitive would not be God's will. More important, if a serious, practicing Christian couple experienced conflict in their marriage, they might intentionally seek a Christian counselor who would be willing to assist them in resolving their differences. They might be very desirous of having the counselor reflect on their problems from religious as well as situational, personal, and interpersonal dynamics. Further, they might want to "work their faith" as well as better understand themselves.

In *encouraging* Christian counseling, counselors affirm the ways in which God is always present to undergird, support, comfort, empower, stand with, and affirm persons in their struggles and in their efforts to face issues and solve their problems. Persons who expect their counselors to give this kind of help see their faith as the very foundation of whatever else they might do to handle their predicaments. They want their counselors to strengthen and reassert the faith they already have. Ideally, they are open to their counselor *correcting* their faith with her or his perceptions of ways in which even their religious beliefs and/or practices needed changing.

In this chapter we have dealt with the expectations of people who seek Christian counseling. We noted how important it is for individuals to know who their counselors are and what type of help they can expect to receive. Christian counseling has structure. It involves professionals and it involves persons who come seeking help. So far, we have only dealt with some of the peripherals. Christian counseling involves method and substance. We turn to these issues in the chapters that follow.

---

1. Paul sought to not be either a burden on or indebted to those he served by maintaining himself through other work. Some counselors cover their fees personally or through the support of Christian churches.

CHAPTER THREE

The Substance of Christian Counseling

ARLIER, WE RECOUNTED THE STORY of the counselor who stated that she would not impose religion on the client who said she was not religious. Someone might well ask that counselor, "If you do not intend to impose 'religion' on this client, what will you impose?" It is widely acknowledged that the day of nondirective counseling has passed. Even Carl Rogers, the initiator of client-centered therapy, who claimed he did not *impose* any of his ideas on those he counseled, did, indeed, influence clients toward his own theory by saying "uh huh" at specific, theory-guided times. He determined when and how persons experienced support for their own self-insight. It is now accepted that all counseling is *impositional*. Every counselor imposes a point of view on those who come for help. All counseling communication is rhetoric—that is, designed to influence clients to reflect on their predicament from a certain perspective. Good counselors adopt a position, state their point of view, and stick to it in their counseling. Psychoanalysts do it. Cognitive behaviorists do it. Christian counselors *should* do it. As the maxim advises, good counselors "plan their work and work their plan."

However, we must admit that, in counseling, imposing a faith or religion may sincerely be perceived by many as somewhat different from imposing a psychological theory. However, there is a significant similarity in what a religious professional (e.g., Christian counselor) and a secular professional (e.g., clinical psychologist) do in their daily work. This similarity can be seen overtly and covertly. *Overtly,* they both have a room where they sit and talk with people after they close the door. Further, they both try to help persons resolve interpersonal and intrapersonal problems through what they say—counseling is "talking therapy," to use Freud's term for what he did. *Covertly,* religious and secular counselors both have a thought-out plan of interaction that determines their diagnosis of the problem and guides the suggestions they make for resolving human predicaments. Although the details of their plans of action may differ, each of their approaches contains the following dimensions:

- An anthropology—a view of the nature of human beings
- A psychopathology—a view of what causes problems in living
- A diagnosis—a conceptualization of the immediate predicament
- A plan for remediation—a sense of what needs to happen for adjustment and/or adaptation to occur
- A goal—an assumption of what healing would look like
- A long-term ideal—a conceptual picture of the good life; their best hope for the future

Thus, Christian counselors, who ground their counseling in the Christian faith, are structurally in a similar business with other counselors, who base their counseling on current psychological theories.

Don Browning and Terry Cooper confirm this observation about the similarity of religious and psychological approaches by contending in their provocative volume *Religious Thought and the Modern Psychologies* (2004) that all models of counseling have deep metaphors. Deep metaphors are those profound and essential presumptions about human life that go far deeper than explicit assertions counselors might make about their theories and/or their approaches. For Browning and Cooper these deep metaphors are implicit synonyms for the dimensions we listed above. Some nonreligious counselors might claim they deal only with nonultimate or transempirical dimensions, but the truth is otherwise. In their book, Browning and Cooper demonstrate conclusively that all counseling theories, religious and nonreligious alike, make metaphysical assumptions about the nature of persons and the goals of counseling that border on being quasi-religious. In fact, these assumptions are implicitly theological. Earlier, Paul Vitz made a similar, but slightly different, observation in his volume *Psychology as Religion: The Cult of Self-worship* (1994). He noted that there was, indeed, a tendency in many contemporary psychological theories to overemphasize a type of individualism that is counter to the basic relational thrust of the Jewish/Christian faith.

Many, however, persist in distinguishing religious communication from counseling. They caution against mixing religion with the psychological theories they teach and learn. A faithful Presbyterian told us that in the training she received she was encouraged to use Transactional Analysis (TA) in the way she responded to those who called her church's emergency hotline for help. She was strongly cautioned against imposing "religion" into the situation. She was told to use religion only with those callers that she knew were religious. It did not seem to matter whether or not those she counseled were believers in Transactional Analysis. It was OK to impose TA on them under the false idea that religion involved nonempirical assumptions but TA did not. They were never asked whether they believed in the tenets of TA.

Her trainers did not seem to realize that both TA (a model less than seventy years old) and her Christian faith (a model two millennia old) dealt with similar, although not necessarily contradictory, implicit dimensions. If Thomas Kuhn (1970) is right about the periodic changes in scientific theories, then many of today's psychological theories of counseling (TA, for example) will give way to newer conceptualizations as time goes on. This has certainly been true for us. Many topics such as "family of origin," "attachment theory," "genograms," and "object relations" were unknown in our training, which took place in the 1960s and 1970s.

We think that such sharp distinctions between religious and psychological theories are ill-advised. Any contention that Christian counselors evangelize whereas secular counselors do not is an illusion, even a delusion. Unfortunately, some professionals seem to have returned to that time in the early part of the twentieth century when religion was a taboo topic that was not to be mixed with social/psychological truths that were assumed to be true for everybody—anywhere, any time. In this line of reasoning, religious faith is thought to be a private matter wherein persons choose to affirm a point of view that is limited to a minority of the population. Somehow it is not realized that each and every psychological theory is also affirmed by only a small part of the population. Only a limited group of counselors are transactional analysts, or cognitive behaviorists, or family system therapists, or object relationists. All counseling theory is affirmed by a select group of counselors. It may be politically correct for counselors to say that they do not impose religion; that is nothing but a politically correct *but untrue* statement for any counselor to make. It is also dangerous because counselors who make such statements often fail to realize that they do, indeed, impose their nonreligious, supposedly secular theories on their clients. And these theories, of whatever kind, are based on quasi-metaphysical, essential presumptions.

In an effort to understand why this tension exists between religious and psychological theories of counseling, Edward C. Lehman Jr. (1974) observed that natural scientists seem to be less antagonistic toward religion than social/behavioral scientists. He explained this phenomenon with a concept called *scholarly distance*. Scholarly distance refers to whether the role a given scientist engages in day to day is similar or different from that played by religious professionals. For example, there is much scholarly distance between the role of a chemist who deals with the chemical composition of dyes and religious professionals who deal with anxiety, sin, redemption, salvation, and Christian living.

There is, however, far less scholarly distance between psychologists and Christian counselors because both are concerned with day-to-day human behavior. Thus, there is much similarity in the roles they play in their everyday lives. Unlike the chemist and religious counselors noted above, secular and religious counselors both talk to people about problems of living. They approach similar life problems from different points of view. The advice given the Presbyterian layperson to not impose religion on those whom she counseled could be seen as competition between two types of counseling providing similar, but different, services. Their narrow definition of scholarly distance made them competitors who argued for the superiority of one theory over another. Thus, there was significant antagonism between religious and nonreligious approaches to dealing with the problems faced by those who answered the emergency telephone calls. According to Lehman, the narrower the social distance (the types of work that they do), the greater the antipathy of different types of professionals (i.e., counselors) toward one another.

One further way of understanding the underlying similarities between religious (in our case Christian) and secular counseling assumptions is to conceive them both as models constructed in the fairly traditional manner of inductive theory development. Such an approach to theory construction suggests that all theories begin with observations of human behaviors (somewhat naively called "facts"). These observations are literally what the term implies—events that are seen, heard, felt, tasted, or smelled. Take, for example, a person who comes for counseling and reports he has become anxious and is unable to sleep. The counselor "hears" this report—it is a "fact." The counselor encourages the person to tell him more. The individual then reports other events surrounding the anxiety and insomnia—more "facts."

In a second step, the counselor looks for *intervening variables* (unstated possible environmental situations or habits that can possibly tie the previous facts together in some meaningful way). At this point in the interaction, both empathy and informed intuition are functioning in the mind of the counselor—*empathy* as the counselor enters into the situation as another human being who could possibly become anxious or have difficulty sleeping in the situation described by the client, and *informed intuition* as the counselor brings to the situation past experience and training in understanding such situations from a given point of view.

Theory construction begins with this move from facts to intervening variables. Both religious and secular counselors begin to reperceive the situation in nonobservable but assumed to be very real terms by using their imagination to transcend empirical reality through the human process of imagination. A nonreligious counselor might use an intervening variable of "disappointment" to tie together the anxiety/insomnia and a failed relationship, whereas a Christian counselor might use "guilt" to make sense of these same feelings.

However, the similarity between theory development in Christian and secular counselors can be observed at this point, where intervening variables begin to be conceived. Both types of counselors utilize unobservable concepts as possible sets of lenses through which to understand the "facts" reported to them in counseling.

The process of theory development proceeds yet another step through what are termed *mediating constructs*. These constructs function to tie together intervening variables at an even higher level of abstraction (i.e., nonobservable yet assumed to be true internal psychodynamic or environmental processes). Mediating constructs are abstract realities assumed to be functioning at a level above the intervening variables and the facts. They refer to intentions or motivations. "Ego crises" or "intergenerational family systems" in psychological theories and "the search for meaning" or "pathological narcissism" in religious counseling theories are examples of mediating constructs. Mediating constructs are often understood to be those *personality variables* inferred in Axis II diagnoses in the *Diagnostic and Statistical Manual of Mental Disorders, DSM IV.*

A given theory that includes facts, intervening variables, and hypothetical constructs is never "proved" to be absolutely true or false, however. In fact, even before postmodernism came to the fore, it was a well-known dictum that what was called "proof" was simply confirmation or support for a given theory. Thus, neither psychological nor religious (i.e., Christian) theories of counseling are ever empirically *true* or *false*. In essence, both contain unobservable concepts for which support, not proof, is demonstrated. The essential explanatory dimensions of their theories (e.g., intervening variables and hypothetical constructs) are abstractions—assumed to be true but empirically nonverifiable. Neither God nor the libido can be seen, tasted, heard, touched, or felt.

All theories are just that—theories. This has now been clearly asserted in postmodernism. Even theologies and Christian distinctives, such as those listed in chapter 1, are theories. No one theory is absolutely more correct than any other. Each theory has the right to a place in the conversation about counseling. Each theory has the responsibility of demonstrating support for, or against, its contentions (cf. Cahoone 1996). We, thereby, offer the tenets of Christian counseling as a theory to be acknowledged and reckoned with in the dialogue among legitimate models of counseling.

What are the intervening variables and mediating constructs of Christian counseling? What is the substance of Christian counseling? The first, and perhaps the most controversial, of these is the concept of God. Benjamin Beit-Hallahmi (1986), in his previously noted discussion about the human experience of transempirical reality, made the important observation that Christians make the assertion that they have experienced the living God. Artists, who also experience transempirical reality, make no such assertion. They believe in *artistic truth* or illusion; Christians believe in *absolute truth*—there is a God!

As with all mediating constructs in all counseling theories, this tenet of the reality of God can neither be logically proved nor disproved. But, as with all such constructs, evidence can lend or not lend support for such a contention. Descending theoretically from the overarching hypothetical construct of God to a set of intervening variables, it is here in the supposed *acts* of God that support for the idea of God can be found.

What is it that Christian counseling contends God does? Stanton L. Jones and Richard E. Butman (1991, 406-9) suggest there are four basic roles God can play in Christian counseling:

- the role of *advocate,*
- the role of *reconciler,*
- the role of *healer,* and
- the role of *director.*[1]

In each of these four roles, it is best that clients perceive this to be the God of the Old and New Testaments with whom they are interacting. This God is the one who created the world, who wants to have human companions, who spoke through the prophets, who sent Jesus to tell the world about him, and who intends that humans find earthly joy and blessing through faithful living. For the Christian, it is not just any God about which affirmations are made. It is the Christian God whose name is love and whose approach is always one of acceptance and endearment.

As *advocate* clients can experience God as supportive, affirming, encouraging, inspiring, energizing, comforting, and consoling.

As *reconciler* clients can experience God as forgiving, confronting, correcting, uniting, inciting, rejoining, and reconciling.

As *healer* clients can experience God as redeeming, quieting, restoring, strengthening, sustaining, resolving, curing, recreating, and undergirding.

As *director* clients can experience God as wisdom-giving, challenging, insight-providing, exciting, stimulating, inspiring, growing, developing, inciting, and a holder of ideals.

Each of these roles of God could be conceived as the intervening variables of Christian counseling. God, the primary foundational hypothetical construct, is experienced as a living presence with clients in their efforts to work through the problems, stress, and challenges of day-to-day living. Clients are presumed to be able to interact with the divine through the transempirical, cognitive process of faith. These intervening variables provide the behind-the-scene impulses that result in observable adjustments/adaptations, which indicate progress is being made in resolving the life predicament brought to the counselor. Thus support, but not proof, is found for the basic theory of Christian counseling. Theologically, Paul Tillich stated it well when he contended that life poses the questions to which faith is the answer (1952).

Of course, it must be acknowledged that this model of the ways that God can be perceived in Christian counseling is idealistic. The God who is experienced or brought to counseling by the client is, by no means, the Christian God whose initial overture is one of support, acceptance, and love. Any presumption that the experience of the God who can be a significant resource for resolution and reformation will be automatic or spontaneous is misguided. Much empathic reflection often is needed to explore difficulties clients might have in allowing the experience of God to be other than overly judgmental, arbitrary, or amorphous. Christian counselors need to avoid any dogmatic presumption that their constructive understandings of how the experience of God should function ideally will be easily incorporated into their clients' efforts to readjust or adapt to the predicaments of their lives.

This chapter has dealt with the *substance* of Christian counseling. In the next chapter, we will turn to a discussion of the *process* of Christian counseling.

---

1. Each of these roles can be buttressed by biblical references. We prefer at this stage in the presentation to argue these in terms of theological functions rather than justifying them via proof texts.

CHAPTER FOUR

The Method of Christian Counseling

I N THE LAST CHAPTER WE CONSIDERED the content or substance of Christian counseling. In this chapter we deal with the method or process of Christian counseling. What is it that Christian counselors actually do? As Erik Berne, the founder of Transactional Analysis, might ask of Christian counselors, "What do you say after you say 'hello?'" In other words, "What do you do when the door is shut and there is nothing but space between you and another person?" Rather than taking a survey of Christian counselors or even listening to audio and/or videotapes of actual sessions, we would like to suggest some models that reflect what we think the method of Christian counseling *should* be.

In one sense, there is nothing unique about what Christian counselors do. They follow the basic two-phase structure of all good counseling: listen first; advise second. In the listening phase, all counselors give persons the chance to describe the dilemma they are facing *from their own point of view*. We italicized "from their own point of view" because that is what it is—the client's own perception of what has gone wrong; their personal sense of the predicament they are facing. This does not mean that counselors accept or agree with what clients say, but they listen in order

- to truly understand clients' perspectives;
- to convince clients that someone cares enough to hear their side of the problem without judging or trying to correct them; and

- to establish a level of trust that will evoke a willingness to join in a search for and to openly consider alternative points of view as well as recommendations the counselor might make.

However, it is probably more in the second phase of counseling that the uniqueness of Christian counseling can be seen. To these distinctives we now turn.

There are four *behavioral* essentials in everyday Christian living: prayer, worship, Scripture reading/study, and witness through service. Christians pray; Christians worship; Christians read and study the Bible; Christians witness to their faith through acts of loving service—each of these essentials is undertaken in an effort to increase and maintain a sense of the presence of God in their daily lives. One formula for understanding how the sense of God's presence functions in daily life is called the 3 Cs. Sensing the presence of God results in *commitment, connection,* and *collaboration.* Christians who sense the presence of God in their daily lives *commit* themselves to loving others as God loves them; *connect* with others in a community of faith; and *collaborate* with God by working toward making the reign of God a reality. These are the ultimate ways in which a sense of God's presence should function in daily life.

A discussion of method could begin with the question of how and whether these four behavioral essentials of prayer, worship, Scripture reading/study, and service can be a part of Christian counselors' efforts to help those whose lives have been disrupted return to commitment, connection, and collaboration. After all, counseling is somewhat unique in its format. Counseling is a meeting off to the side of daily existence. At times, counseling has been called "paid friendship." Samuel Southard (1989) calls it "the wisdom of God in the context of friendship." Counseling is different from church. Often, Christian counselors are not ordained nor are they evangelists. Should they pray for or with those they counsel, accompany them to worship services, involve them in the church, or help them plan some acts of service? Should they lead them in a study of the biblical passages that might apply to the issues they are facing? The answer is probably yes and no.

The yes and no answers to whether praying, worshiping, reading/studying Scripture, and planning acts of service with clients should be a part of Christian counseling could be grouped under three basic approaches: *explicit*, *implicit*, and *intentional*. The explicit approach basically answers yes; the implicit approach basically answers no; and the intentional approach basically answers yes and no to this query.

Why Christians Do What They Do

Before describing in more detail the explicit, implicit, and intentional alternatives, we would like to return to a phrase we used earlier that depicts *why* Christians pray, worship, read/study Scripture, and witness through acts of service. We said that Christians engage in these behaviors "in an effort to increase and maintain the sense of God in their daily lives." It would seem important, then, to determine whether Christian counselors should have this same goal of increasing and maintaining the sense of God among their clients.

Our answer would be a resounding yes. In fact, we would contend that increasing and maintaining a sense of God might be the *master* motive in all Christian counseling. We suspect that our contention of increasing and maintaining a sense of God in daily life as the master motive in Christian counseling might need some elaboration, lest such a statement be disregarded as too obvious or too trite. Our justification for this assertion lies in our understanding of basic psychology. We believe every human being has the capacity to experience transempirical and/or essential reality. As we have noted, synonyms for this capacity are "imagination," "aesthetic appreciation," "spirituality," and "fantasy" (cf. Winnicott 1971, Beit-Hallahmi 1986). In other words, every human being has the capacity to be *spiritual*—to transcend and experience a dimension of life above that of the five senses; that is, empirical, sensate reality. We contend that this can mean that everyone has the capacity to experience a sense of God in his or her life.

We use the word *capacity* here in a technical sense. Capacity does not mean "instinct," or else everybody's experience and expression of transcendent and/or essential reality would occur automatically and be the same from person to person. Clearly, this is not the case. Nor does capacity mean "basic drive," or else everyone would experience the spirituality impulse just like everyone gets hungry and eats food. There are definitely people who report they have never had a spiritual experience nor do they feel they want it. Spirituality is a "capacity," a "native ability," an "option"—humans can have it, if they want—but they do not "have to" (cf. Malony 2001).

When we contend that Christian counselors intend to increase and maintain the sense of God in those who come to them for help, we are asserting that "the sense of God" is a transempirical, imaginative, spiritual experience that people have to want and to seek. Neither clients, nor their counselors, have ever *seen* God. God is not experienced empirically, in spite of those who rarely report hearing God speak to them, as did Samuel, or see visions, as did Isaiah. Since God is, as we have said earlier, the prime mediating construct of Christian counseling theory, experiencing a sense of God would naturally appear to be a basic therapeutic goal.

Several caveats must be kept in mind. First, we admit, from the viewpoint of Christian faith, God is more than people's experience. We agree with that truth. But people do not come to counseling to *study* God, they come to counseling to *encounter* God. And the only means through which humans can encounter God is through transempirical and/or essential experience. Of course, God is more than the human experience of God; and in counseling, Christian counselors assert that God provides very specific options for resolving individual problems—as we noted in the previous chapter. Whoever else God is and whatever else God does in the world, in counseling the Christian God is "our refuge and strength, a very present help in trouble" (Psalm 46:1).

A second caveat is that transempirical and/or essential experience is not self-explanatory—it calls for interpretation. There is no direct one-to-one connection between this experience and the experience of God. This is where religion comes into the picture. It can be said that whereas "spirituality is the experience, religion is the explanation." When explanatory words are put to transempirical and/or essential experience, religion interprets the experience, be it Buddhist, Christian, or other.

There are illustrations of this need for words that explain spiritual experience in the Bible. Moses asked God for the words to put to his burning bush experience. "Say to the Israelites, 'The LORD, the God of your fathers—the God of Abraham, the God of Isaac and the God of Jacob—has sent me to you'" (Exodus 3:15 NIV). This is religion, that is, words that explain spiritual experience. Eli reinterpreted a spiritual situation and told Samuel to reply when next he heard the voice, "Speak LORD, for your servant is listening" (1 Samuel 3:9 NIV). Spirituality became religion for Samuel. Similarly, Paul's words to the Athenians on Mars Hill explained, or reinterpreted, their spiritual experience. Paul said, "Men of Athens! I see that in every way you are very religious. For as I walked around and looked carefully at your objects of worship, I even found an altar with this inscription: TO AN UNKNOWN GOD. Now what you worship as something unknown I am going to proclaim to you" (Acts 17:22-23 NIV).

Religion is the term given to such proclamatory, inspiring, explanatory words for transempirical and/or essential spiritual experience. It is our conviction that spiritual experience only becomes functionally powerful for persons when it becomes religion—those explanatory words that give substance and intent to the force behind the experience. These words, which we have called intervening variables and hypothetical constructs, function to induce a repeat of the experience and give meaning to it.

Faith is action based on these understandings. To "live by faith" means to be motivated intentionally and self-consciously in one's thoughts, words, feelings, and actions by the "words" one has ascribed to the experience of transempirical and essential reality. An illustration of this can be seen among those who routinely read *The Upper Room* devotional guide. The "words" of the reading for a given day evoke a subliminal memory of the reader's Christian faith heritage and inspire them to reexperience the presence of God in the moments that follow. All ritual functions in this manner—be it that of a Benedictine-guided retreat, a Sunday morning Presbyterian service, or a charismatic group prayer.

The import of these caveats is to reaffirm our contention that "increasing and maintaining a sense of God" is, indeed, the master motive for Christian counselors and that prayer, worship, the reading/study of Scripture, and service might be important means by which Christian counselors accomplish this goal.

Explicit, Implicit, and Intentional Approaches

We have noted that the prime means through which humans encounter God is through spiritual experience that is informed by religion (i.e., the words of the Christian faith). Prayer, worship, Scripture reading/study, and acts of loving service could be understood as the basic methods through which to induce such experience. In answer to the question of *when* and *how* this can be done, we suggest three approaches: explicit, implicit, and intentional.

Explicit Approach

The explicit approach to Christian counseling would incorporate each of these behaviors as interventions regardless of whether they were requested by the client and/or directly relevant to the problem being addressed. This explicit approach assumes that clients would expect a Christian counselor to use Christian resources. If this does not happen, clients take the treatment as less important and become confused. In fact, where explicit resources are not used, clients may feel a fiduciary relationship has been violated and may wonder whether or not the counselor is competent. Friendship without some sharing of the wisdom of God would not be Christian counseling, according to Southard's (1989) understanding.

Siang-Yang Tan (1996) has been a proponent of this approach. He would begin sessions with prayer and would not hesitate to include prayer within the session at critical times. Further, Tan suggests that the Christian counselor should have a set of Bible passages that clients ought to read and study during the counseling hour or between sessions. These passages would be selected as applicable to the situation being dealt with in the sessions. Although discussion of these passages would be appropriate during the counseling session, interpretation should be limited to their applicability for solving problems or increasing an awareness of God. The counseling session should not become a study session; but the basic assumption is that "all neurotic anxiety is grounded in basic anxiety," as Paul Tillich might contend.

The explicit approach can be both reassuring and confrontational. Counselors can point to many biblical references that reassure clients of the love, comfort, and presence of God. However, this approach can be confrontational when they point to passages that indicate God's judgment. When used by an empathic counselor both alternatives can be constructive. Our basic preference is that *all* biblical references to God should begin with the reassurance of

God's love. The model exemplified by the Nouwen story of giving a blessing told in chapter 1 is the ideal.

Planning acts of loving service is most often done late in counseling when clients have gained some self-confidence in dealing with their life predicaments and are able to conceive of ways to express their faith. Some explicit counselors think they have not been truly helpful if counseling ends without their clients finding ways to express their faith in loving service of others. It has been contended that "wholeness" should lead to "holiness" but this does not always happen (cf. Malony 1995). Again and again, Christian counselors have to be content with clients leaving without discussing how best to grow in their faith.

One problematic aspect of the explicit approach pertains to worship. Worship usually means church. And church implies contact with clients outside of counseling. Suggesting to clients that they should go to church is one thing. Accompanying them to church is another. The trust and confidentiality that are essential for counseling can easily be threatened in public situations. Nevertheless, the issue is not whether, but how to encourage participation in the life of a church (i.e., worship) for those counselors who adopt the explicit approach. They would not automatically hesitate to accompany clients to church, although they would strongly prefer to not have contact with clients outside of the counseling hour. We will discuss referral in more detail in a later chapter, but one strategic approach that has been used by explicit counselors is to have a group of ministers who will agree to incorporate clients into their fellowships.

Implicit Approach

Interestingly enough, Siang-Yan Tan, who is a strong supporter of the explicit approach cautions against the use of the four Christian essentials unless clients agree to their inclusion in counseling. Tan's caution is a natural segue into the opposite alternative. This implicit approach regards the use of overt religious resources as intrusive and impositional unless the client specifically requests it or unless it is directly applicable to a religious issue in the problem being dealt with by the client. Even then, it is preferable not to be overtly religious. Counselors should not impose their religion on unsuspecting clients. Instead, requests by clients to include religious resources should be explored and should become a part of the counseling process itself.

Being reluctant to use prayer, worship, Scripture reading/study, or service planning explicitly in counseling does not mean that implicit Christian counselors affirm any less than their explicit counterparts the goal of increasing and maintaining a sense of God's presence in daily life. They just believe it can be done more effectively if done covertly and indirectly.

In fact, those who take the implicit approach often affirm strongly an *incarnational* methodology and presume that the counselor becomes "Christ" to the client through modeling the love of God in a manner that can be seen and experienced interpersonally. Thomas C. Oden (1966) wrote persuasively about this option. Writing during a period where the therapeutic conditions of empathy, warmth, and congruence were being emphasized, Oden contended that where this kind of atmosphere was provided for the client, there the grace of God was revealed. Christian counselors who use the implicit approach attempt to communicate by example more than by content. It may be remembered that earlier we discounted "incarnational" presumptions on the part of counselors. Perhaps we should have contended that we did not agree with exclusive claims that resulted in counselors seeing no need to ever overtly state their basic convictions. We still think Christian counselors should be clear in their own self-understanding about the ultimate validity of clients finding their security in the experience of the presence of God and be willing to proclaim this in printed as well as public statements about themselves. The issue is not whether, but when and how, this should be made a part of counseling.

This issue is reminiscent of the distinction that has been made between "do and tell" and "tell and do" foreign mission theory. Those who adopt the implicit approach to counseling would prefer to "do" counseling and "tell" about their Christian faith later, if ever. Those who adopt the explicit approach would tend to "tell" about their Christian faith as they "do" their counseling.

If we think of the explicit approach as emphasizing *content*, then the implicit approach emphasizes *context*. There is little doubt that counselors, not theories, are the crucial, most important determinants of counseling outcomes. In fact, counselors have been rated as more crucial to healing than the specific methods they use. Often clients describe their counselors' style but are unable to name their theoretical approach.

In regard to worship, implicit Christian counselors would never accompany their clients to church. They might be supportive of church involvement if they felt the church was helpful and understanding of life struggles. As counseling progressed, planning for acts of service would be good if, and only if, clients brought up the issue. Implicit Christian counselors are likely to be much more trustful of the healing dynamic within their clients than those who adopt the explicit approach.

It would probably be encouraged and acceptable for those taking both the implicit and the explicit approaches to actively pray for their clients, read and study Scripture, be involved in church life, and personally witness to their faith by engaging in acts of loving service over and beyond their vocations of counseling.

Intentional Approach

The intentional approach to using prayer, worship, Scripture reading/study, and service planning in counseling cuts across both the explicit and implicit modalities. It affirms an approach that is significantly different from them. In a sense, it deals more with context and intention than with the question of the overt or covert use of religious specifics. The intentional method is directed toward setting the stage and/or rekindling a state of mind before, during, and after the counseling hour. It allows the overt use of prayer, worship, and Scripture reading where appropriate as well as emphasizes the importance of the covert communication of faith through the counselor's demeanor. However, the major goal of increasing and maintaining the sense of God is accomplished by clearly, intentionally, and explicitly calling the client's attention to the divine context in which the event occurs. The counselor does not wait for the client to request this, but explains to the client the format that will be followed. This is similar to psychoanalysts who tell clients to lie on the couch and free associate and Gestalts who tell clients they will expect them to be ready to identify a concern when they open the meeting with the words, "What do you want to work on today?" Likewise, intentional Christian counseling sets the environmental conditions under which their sessions will be organized.

The intentional approach involves a set of steps that we feel take into consideration the best facets of both the explicit and the implicit models at the same time that it structures Christian counseling within a unique contextual modality (cf. Malony 1995). Intentional Christian counseling begins with the overarching assumption that the counseling event occurs within the context of *Heilsgeschickte* or "holy history"—the work of God in the world, both in the lives of individual and groups of persons and in the lives of nations. Counseling moments are part of God's efforts to restore, redeem, and lead the world toward a divine end through the talents of counselors and the healing of clients. God has ordained that the primary way God's will be accomplished is through human relationships—particularly those interactions where people consciously intend to do God's will. Christian counseling becomes a prime example of witness and worship. It is both a renewing of the experience of the presence of God for client and counselor and an example of loving service in God's name.

Action Step 1: Prayer for Guidance

Prior to each session, it is not uncommon for counselors to look over their notes to remind themselves of the issues on which their clients are working. In this first action step, intentional counselors add to their preparation a prayer to God for guidance. They intentionally remind and reorient themselves to the holy context in which counseling is to take place. They recommit themselves to following the leadership of God as far as possible in what they say and how they relate in the session. They intentionally open themselves up to their own sense of God and ask for skill in listening and in leading clients into the next steps in their healing and restoration. They commit themselves to being channels of God's grace and ask for strength to be alert and attentive during the counseling session. Likewise, they pray that those they are about to counsel will be open to God's presence. Since this is a moment in holy history, the prayer concludes with an expression of hope that the counseling hour will contribute toward making this world become the "kingdom of our Lord and of his Messiah" (Revelation 11:15 NRSV).

Action Step 2: Invitation

After counselors prepare for the session by praying, they bring their clients into the room and invite them to acknowledge that God is in the room with them. Clients need to be reminded that they, too, stand in the presence of God, who has a will for how they can best be helped. In a process that will be repeated each time they meet, Christian counselors can invite clients by saying, "Join me in a silent prayer as we ask God to guide our time together." After a short time has passed the counselor may say, "The Lord be with you." These are the ancient words that begin Christian worship. These words are a way of saying, "May God be present with us during our time together to lead and guide your sharing and your response to what I say. May God's will be done in what we do and say."

In the intentional approach clients are, in effect, trained in this format. They learn this procedure. Note that this is done quite apart from whether clients are Christian or request this. It is part of the way Christian counseling is intentionally structured. In response to the invitation, the client(s) learns to reply, "And may God be with you, also." This is the client's admonition to the counselor to listen to God during the session as he or she guides the interaction. It is also a way for clients to say they will listen for God and they hope counselors will do the same.

Action Step 3: Proclamation

This third step is a clear statement of the unique context in which the Christian counseling session occurs. The counselor proclaims, "The risen Christ is with us," to which clients are invited to respond, "Thanks be to God." The intention here is to affirm the most profound of Christian assertions, namely that Jesus Christ has risen from the dead and is present in the counseling session. Most important, it is a recognition that Jesus stands ready to support, encourage, and assist the client in the good, but hard, work of counseling.

Christians worship a triune God: Father, Son, and Holy Spirit. God the Father has a will for this counseling session, but Jesus mediates God's will for human existence. It is crucial for clients to know in their hearts that Jesus, who experienced what it was like to be a human being, is actually there to stand alongside them as they work through the problems of their own existence. This is the reason they say, "Thanks be to God." The Almighty is not some far-off divinity, but a living presence in the form of Jesus the Christ. By responding, "Thanks be to God," they are acknowledging the "good news" that Jesus will be their constant companion. He is one who fully understands and who has the power to heal their thinking and their relationships.

Of course, the maxim "saying doesn't make it so" is definitely true when we state that the risen Christ is present in the counseling room. It is one thing for the counselor and client to hope that God (i.e., the Lord) will be with each of them during the session and another thing to assert with any conviction that Jesus is there. It is almost like asking clients to affirm a vision or a hallucination. Further, clients may have confusion in their mind about such an idea and find imagining Jesus as present very difficult. We recommend that the statement about the risen Christ not be belabored—just stated and left without discussion unless and until clients bring it up. The import of that affirmation will become apparent as counseling progresses. After all, as changes in behavior are considered, the presence of Jesus may be experienced as supportive and encouraging in a manner that becomes especially helpful. Initially, it may be best to approach it in a manner similar to the way John Wesley advised dealing with prayer. He suggested: first pray because you have to and sometime in the future you will pray because you must.

Action Step 4: The Creative Middle

In the intentional approach, the actual work of restoration and healing takes place after steps one, two, and three have set the context for the session. This is termed the *creative middle*. It is creative in a theological and practical sense. In a theological sense, it is creative because during the middle time of counseling *re-creation* occurs—human life is remade and redeemed from its problematic and fallen state. In a practical sense, it is creative because during this middle part of counseling the problems of human adjustment and adaptation are worked out in a manner that increases the possibility for happiness as well as fulfillment.

During these middle moments of the counseling session, counselors use one or more of the extant psychological theories that provide understanding, explanation, and remediation for the various psychopathologies of human existence and interaction. It may seem surprising that we affirm the value of nonreligious, secular perspectives. However, we depict these theories based on average, social adjustment models that describe ways persons can interrelate day by day with one another in supportive and fulfilling manners. We define everyday adjustment as not being a danger to self or others, or being gravely disabled. Many of the existing psychological theories of counseling are based on behavioral dynamics that go beyond these three dangers, which simply describe learning processes that are neither good nor bad—they just are. They often include procedures for regaining self-adjustment and adaptation. Christian counseling theory is a normative, aspirational, and theological model that undergirds these efforts as well as goes beyond them by defining joy as the strength to face stress and to live mercifully and justly as one "walk[s] humbly with . . . God" (Micah 6:8).

Both Christian and social adjustment theories are appropriate for understanding human experience and alleviating human distress. The creative middle of each counseling session acknowledges this. In fact, Christian counseling affirms the value of many psychological, secular models as illustrative of the conviction that "all truth is God's truth." Christian counseling is vitally interested in the happiness and joy that can come from human insight, adjustment, and mutual interaction. Whereas the Christian model talks forcefully about aspiring to be just and merciful, its only model for what goes wrong is sin—willful violation of the will of God for life. This is a good and profound insight that Reinhold Niebuhr and others have contended is at the root of all anxiety. However, a number of currently available nonreligious, learning-based counseling models have a much more complex and detailed understanding of what goes wrong in human life. We consider some of these in more detail in the Applications section of this book. In spite of the fact that the assumptions about the ultimate goals of living that some of the models make (cf. Browning and Cooper 2004) are devoid of the theological presumptions Christians consider important, their basic analyses of human dynamics are very insightful in helping clients understand themselves—not only their human frailty and sinfulness but also their potential for strength and salvation.

One current cognitive-behavioral model is illustrative of this use of existing nonreligious, secular approaches during the creative middle of intentional Christian counseling. David Hays (2003) advocates Acceptance Commitment Therapy (ACT). He suggests that many people aspire to unbridled happiness and seek counseling when they should realize that human life always involves suffering, compromise, and failure. In his therapy he encourages clients to *accept* life more realistically and to find joy by *committing* themselves to some higher goals that will provide meaning for them in their daily life. Thus ACT would be a very compatible secular model to the ultimate aspirations of Christian counseling gained through prayer, Scripture reading/study, worship, and service.

Christian counselors can use these models while counseling in the creative middle. In fact, much of the insight that counselees gain after they have become reassured that they are loved and supported by God, as well as befriended by the risen Christ, will be found in these secular models. On this topic, Christian counselors can refer to Stanton Jones and Richard Butman's book *Modern Psychotherapies: A Comprehensive Christian Analysis* (1991). These authors evaluated which secular theories are most compatible with the Christian faith. It could be said that Christian theology deals more with the origin and destiny of human life while psychological theory generally deals more with day-to-day human functioning.

Of course, there are some foundational differences in the two approaches, as we have noted earlier. Yet they need not be contradictory. The reasoning of Galileo illustrates this approach. He contended that his early laws of mechanical motion (e.g., the speed of a ball is determined by the strength of the force pushing it and the degree of the angle of the incline plane) were no threat to Christian faith. He suggested he was merely describing how the world moves, not why it moved or where it was going (cf. Malony 1995, 13). Although it is a bit of an overstatement, modern psychological theories deal with *how* humans behave; Christian theology deals with *why*. One is descriptive; the other is prescriptive. Suffice it to say that in the creative middle step of the intentional use of prayer, worship, and Scripture reading, Christian counselors utilize these and other current psychological methods to help clients achieve an understanding of their behavior.

It is important to remember that insight alone does not heal. Healing results from doing something constructive with the insight one achieves. The maxim is, "Although insight does not heal, there is no healing without insight." What clients do with insight in Christian counseling is very often facilitated by "increasing and maintaining a sense of God." The sense of God that is achieved through intentional Christian counseling can be brought to the challenge that is required for healing to occur. As noted in the previous chapter, we experience God as advocate, reconciler, healer, and director. In energizing the sense of God in each of these roles, clients become emboldened to engage in different behaviors in their daily lives. Behavior changes life. Insight helps, but practice of new behavior is the key to healing.

Action Step 5: Committing Clients to God

Christian counseling in the intentional approach concludes with a benediction. A benediction is always a prayer for sustaining the presence of God in the hours between sessions. Psychologists call this the problem of "generalization," that is, how to maintain the insight gained, the commitment made, and the new behavior sustained in the days and hours when clients are on their own. The benediction recontextualizes the client's situation as living with God and walking with Jesus Christ. The client is not alone. Almost any of the great benedictions will do. Here are a couple of adaptations we find helpful:

> May the Lord bless you and keep you; may the Lord make His face to shine upon you and give you peace.

> May God the Father who is creating you, God the Son who is redeeming you, and God the Holy Spirit who is sustaining you, bless, preserve and keep you until we meet again.

These, as well as other benedictions, state clearly the faith that God is at work in people's lives. As Romans 8:28 (NIV) states, "In all things God works for the good of those who love him." At the end of the counseling session, remind people that if they "love" God by remembering God throughout the day, God will, indeed, work through all things (i.e., their problems) for good.

A special issue arises in the aftermath of these benedictions. Whereas the first two explicit behaviors (prayer and Bible reading) can take place *within*, as well as *outside*, the counseling session, worship should, by definition, take place *outside*. Worship should always take place at church. We use the word *at* advisedly because we do not mean to imply *at* a building. We do mean *with* other Christians as they seek to encourage, inspire, guide, support, and direct one another in the living of the Christian life. No matter what behavioral decisions counselees make in the creative middle of intentional counseling, they still need the inspiration, affirmation, and undergirding that come through involvement in the church. Both times of worship and times of fellowship provide the social support that is always needed for counseling to be effective in handling the stress of life.

The critical question for Christian counselors is, How can worship (i.e., church involvement) be recommended and guaranteed? Should the counselor take persons to church, as the explicit approach might advocate? Or should the counselor remain passive and never involve him or herself in this way, as the implicit approach might advocate? And, if one takes the intentional approach, how might involving persons in church be affected, since such behavior always occurs outside the counseling hour?

One approach could be for the Christian counselor to amass a list of pastors who might be open to incorporating counselees into their church life when counselees are referred to them. This is tantamount to having these pastors become cocounselors of persons. This approach has been described in the book by Phyllis Hart and Ralph Osborne entitled *Concurrent Counseling: An Integrative Approach to Counseling by Pastor and Psychologist* (1988). Persons who come for counseling should be advised that this kind of cocounseling might be involved so that they are not surprised when it occurs.

The intentional approach to the inclusion of prayer, worship, Scripture reading and study, and service appears to include the best of the explicit and implicit models; yet it adds another dimension that puts counseling within a Christian environment. It contextualizes Christian counseling as a specifically religious event.

This chapter has dealt with the question of method in Christian counseling. Prayer, worship, Scripture reading/study, and witnessing to faith through loving service of others were identified as the four behavior essentials. Among Christians, the goal behind these behaviors is to increase and sustain a sense of God in daily Christian living. These objectives are affirmed as the master motives for Christian counseling. Three approaches (explicit, implicit, and intentional) were described. The intentional approach was presented as the option for combining the best of the other two and for adding a contextual component that make this approach the preferred option.

CHAPTER FIVE

Faith Assessment in Christian Counseling

THE CHRISTIAN FAITH OF MANY is like the fallen blooms of the Jacaranda trees in the early summer in Southern California. The trees are everywhere. They cover the streets and the sidewalks with their lavender bossoms. One woman was heard to exclaim, "You can't avoid stepping on these fallen Jacaranda blooms. They are like a carpet that covers the earth once a year. You step on them on the sidewalk and they leave a stain. Unless you scrape your shoes vehemently, you will carry them into your house where they will stain your floors or your carpet. What can we do? Do we not need a sweeper of some kind to go over all the land each night and clean the streets, the yards, and the sidewalks?"

This seasonal condition of the Jacaranda blossoms covering the earth in Southern California could be compared to the traditional Christian religious ground on which citizens of the United States walk throughout summer, fall, and winter, as well as spring. Many accept this faith carpet and are pleased that they can look down and always see that it is there. They are comforted by it and even attend rallies to honor it. Others, however, have begun to complain about it. "Why can't we find a sweeper to cleanse the earth of this contaminant that stains the ground on which we walk and that seeps into our houses on the soles of our shoes?"

In his book *All Over but the Shoutin'* (1997), Rick Bragg

describes this kind of faith carpet on which everybody walked in rural Alabama, where he grew up. In commenting on his mother's report that when his estranged father called, "mostly he just wanted to talk about the Lord," Bragg wrote, "I guess it is what you do if you grow up with warnings of damnation ringing from every church door and radio station and family reunion, in a place where total strangers walk up to you at the Piggly Wiggly and ask if you are Saved. Even if you deny that faith, rebuke it, you still carry it around with you like some half-forgotten Indian head penny you keep in your pocket for luck" (p. 8).

However, those who come to Christian counselors should be prepared to do more than be casual walkers who occasionally wander into a church or who have good friends they meet there for Sunday school lessons. They should expect to do more than simply assume a Christian counselor will not charge as much as others or be willing to perform some kind of holy quick fix. Using the metaphor of the Jacaranda blossoms, they should expect to look up to the limbs of the Jacaranda tree and ask, "Where do those blossoms come from?" In other words, instead of looking for a miracle, they might look up to the God above it all and sincerely ask, "What might faith in the Christian revelation truly mean for everyday life?"

Such a search for the meaning of Christian faith can provide a personal foundation for "working the faith" in the midst of the stresses and strains of life that bring persons to counseling in the first place. Christian counseling should provide an opportunity to explore faith in a manner that goes far beyond just walking on the carpet of faith on which most people walk. Christian counselors see this endeavor as the opportunity to explore the ways in which their clients' faith walk is working and ways in which improvement can be cultivated.

To extend this metaphor further, it is well known that walking is good for you. Most people like to walk. They walk to their cars; they walk in the shopping malls; they walk to the movies; they walk from their cars to church; they walk to school; they walk around their homes; they walk to the bus. Walking is what we do. Instead of suggesting an alternative way of thinking about *what* one walks on, the very act of *walking* itself might provide further insight into exploring Christian faith.

Although almost everyone walks to some degree, there are some folk who become very earnest about walking. They walk to increase or maintain their health. They plan their walking. They schedule their walks. Walking is the way they exercise. They are not casual about walking; they are dedicated to doing more than walking for pleasure. Christian counseling might be conceived as becoming serious about the "walk of faith."

These different types of walkers could be compared to different types of Christians. Unfortunately, many who come for counseling are first-level walkers. They want to use their routine faith walking to function intensely and effectively when they face problems in living. The task of Christian counseling is to help walkers become hikers. If Christian faith is to become more than words, that is, faith that works, then counselors will need to help persons

1. assess the level of their understanding,
2. strengthen their comprehension,
3. put their faith to work,
4. design behaviors that will be supported by faith, and
5. experience support in their faith endeavors.

This outline of counseling work may sound strangely like spiritual guidance, but the resemblance goes only so far. In fact, the typical beginning point for spiritual guidance is significantly different from that of counseling. Persons who want to deepen an already vibrant faith most often seek *spiritual guidance;* persons who are experiencing distress in daily life most often seek *counseling.* The motivation for spiritual guidance is development; the motivation for counseling is readjustment. Although guidance can be a part of counseling, usually counselees want help more than guidance. They want deliverance, not instruction.

On occasion, clients' distress is directly related to their Christian faith. Faith that used to work can be eroded by doubt. Participation in religious activities can wane with family transitions. New types of spiritual experiences can confound old habits.

A friend of ours left her eighteen-month-old daughter with in-laws while she and her husband took a short weekend cruise in the Bahamas. On Saturday night the daughter choked to death on her nightgown while trying to get out of the crib. As our friend's husband bent over his dead daughter he prayed for a miracle. His daughter did not return to life. From that day on he never set foot in church again. Before this tragedy he was a very involved Christian. This illustrates only one of many "spiritual emergencies" that David Lukoff, Robert Turner, and Frank Lu (1992) listed in their recommendation that *The Diagnostic and Statistical Manual of Mental Disorders DSM-IV* include a "V" code for identifying "religious and spiritual problems" that might be brought to counseling.[1]

Assessing Christian Faith

Assessing the counselee's level of understanding of Christian faith is the first step that counselors might take toward helping persons make religion more functional in their daily lives. On one hand, one could start by asking the counselee if he or she believed one of the classic statements of faith such as the Apostles' or Nicene creeds. But this would only assess their *beliefs*. On the other hand, one could ask how often they went to church or read the Bible. But this would only assess *behavior*. What is needed is a way that combines the two: their faith and how they put their beliefs into action. We call this *functional theology*.

A way to assess functional theology was suggested by the Menninger Foundation psychologist Paul W. Pruyser. In his classic *The Minister as Diagnostician* (1976), Pruyser proposes a set of dimensions that can be combined into a measure of Christian religious maturity. Christian maturity gives Christian counselors the telos of counseling. Said another way, knowing what religious maturity looks like can provide the norms or standards against which clients' behavior can be evaluated. The following is a discussion of Pruyser's dimensions. The definitions of optimal Christian functioning are from Malony (1989, 12).

Awareness of God: Christians for whom their faith is optimally functioning are aware that they have been created by God and made in God's image. While recognizing their own capabilities, they recognize their dependence on God for strength. They have a realistic awareness of their own limitations but do not deny their responsibility to utilize their abilities in fulfilling God's will. They worship

God as an expression of their reverence and love for God. They pray as a means of communing with God and expressing their concerns honestly with God.

Acceptance of God's Grace and Steadfast Love: Christians for whom their faith is optimally functioning know God loves them unconditionally. They accept God's love and forgiveness as an impetus for new life and responsible action. God's love gives them the ability to find meaning in the suffering and difficulty of their lives. They trust the goodness of God.

Being Repentant and Responsible: Christians for whom their faith is optimally functioning take responsibility for their own feelings and actions. They do not deny, however, the influence of other factors, such as the environment, on the difficulties they may face and the sins they commit. They accept their inner impulses as part of their humanness, yet realize a proclivity toward evil. They are able to request and accept forgiveness from others without feeling threatened or self-depreciating. They forgive others without continuing to experience resentment toward them.

Knowing God's Leadership and Direction: Christians for whom their faith is optimally functioning trust in God's leadership yet accept their own role in the process of making decisions. They express an optimistic yet realistic hope in God's control of life. They have a strong sense of their own place in making the will of God come to pass. This identity of being God's stewards gives deep meaning to their lives.

Involvement in Organized Religion: Christians for whom their faith is functioning optimally engage in regular and systematic involvement with other Christians in worship, prayer, study, and service. By their behavior, they evidence commitment to organized religion. They know the value of group identity and involvement. They join with others in trying to grow in their spiritual understanding and faithful behavior.

Experiencing Fellowship: Christians for whom their faith is optimally functioning experience fellowship at various levels of intimacy and involvement with other believers. They identify themselves with other members of the family of God in local communities and throughout the world. They rejoice with others in knowing themselves as those who have accepted God's invitation to live as followers of Christ, and have a sense of fellowship with Christians everywhere. They see the world and all people in it as part of God's good creation, to be respected, honored, and loved.

Being Ethical: Christians for whom their faith is optimally functioning follow their ethical principles in a flexible but committed manner. Religious faith underlies their total behavior. Religious life is inevitably moral life. They show a concern for peace, love, and justice both in personal and social areas of life. They are concerned for individual responsibility and social justice. They live with the sense that they are loving God through their vocations.

Affirming Openness in Faith: Christians for whom their faith is optimally functioning experience their religion as the prime directive in their lives. They spend a significant amount of time discussing, reading, and thinking about their faith. They attempt to grow and increase in their understanding of their faith. Although they express confidence in and commitment to the Christian faith, they nevertheless are tolerant of others' points of view and are willing to examine others' beliefs in an honest manner. They are open to critiques of Christ. Their faith is complex.

Pruyser (1976) suggested a number of questions that might be used to probe the faith development of those who come for counseling. He concluded that counselors might develop a profile of strengths and weaknesses in an effort to determine areas of faith that might be used as assets in treatment, as well as facets of faith that could be used in recommendations for new behavior.

We have developed a structured interview and a paper-and-pencil inventory using Pruyser's model, which we have described in this chapter. These measures assess Christian religious maturity along the eight dimensions noted above. The scores that counselors derive from these measures provide profiles that can be used in the counseling process to assist clients in increasing the presence of God in their lives. Further, these measures, called the *Religious Status Interview* and the *Religious Status Inventory,* can help clients identify areas where they might focus on increasing their religious maturity. The interview will take about an hour and the inventory can be completed in a half hour. Both have been used in a number of empirical studies and have been found to have adequate validity and reliability. They should always be a part of the counseling process and shared with clients in an empathic, non-judgmental fashion.[2]

Of course, it would be extremely rare, almost theoretically impossible, for an individual to obtain a perfect score on each of these measures even if it were assumed that the scores had a one-to-one relationship with absolute Christian religious maturity, that is, a faultless walk of faith. However, in using such assessment tools as these, Christian counselors need to have an ideal delineation in their minds about what a perfect walk of faith might look like, that is, what might be the appearance of truly functioning theology in the way persons live their lives. The following is a working model that we find useful.

> Mature Christians are those who have identity, integrity, and inspiration. They have "identity" in that their self-understanding is that they are children of God—created by God and destined to live according to a divine plan. They have "integrity" in that their daily lives are lived in the awareness that they have been redeemed by God's grace from the guilt of sin and that they can freely respond to God's will in the present. They have "inspiration" in that they live with the sense that God is available to sustain, comfort, encourage, and direct their lives on a daily basis. These dimensions of maturity relate to belief in God the Father, God the Son, and God the Holy Spirit. They pertain to the Christian doctrines of creation, redemption, and sanctification. They provide the foundation for practical daily living. (Malony 1996, 250)

That any human being would ever be able to attain and sustain such a self-understanding as this might be possible but it is highly improbable. Nor are we convinced that the behaviors measured by the Religious Status Interview and Inventory are a complete assessment of Christian living. Further, we do not want to imply that even if such self-understanding and behavior were possible that persons would, thereby, never experience anxiety, depression, uncertainty, or disappointment. Even Jesus, who attained this absolute ideal, met with disaster and death. We are convinced, however, of the power of Christian "faithing" to work in, through, above, and beyond existence to provide ways to surmount all the predicaments of life. Our method for assuring that the counseling hour is encompassed by affirming the will of God and the presence of Christ is a model of this conviction. As we suggested in this chapter, following these affirmations in which Christian counselors use one or more of the current therapeutic approaches for resolving intrapersonal and interpersonal problems provides a means for achieving the final goal of Christian maturity.

1. See H. Newton Malony, "A Response to Brun," *Journal of Pastoral Care and Counseling* 59, no. 5 (2005): 449-51, and H. Newton Malony, "The V62.89 Code of the DSM-IV-R: Boone and Bane for Christian Psychologists," *Theology News and Notes* 53, no. 1 (2005): 10-11, 25.

2. A packet of articles that report the development and standardization of these measures can be obtained by writing to H. Newton Malony, 650 West Harrison Ave., Claremont, CA 91711 or by sending an e-mail to hnewtonm@yahoo.com.

CHAPTER SIX

Counseling That Fosters Forgiveness

OUT OF THE TRUTH AND RECONCILIATION Commission in South Africa, a story emerges that is told and retold. It is a parable about the tension between reconciliation and truth, between easy forgiving and authentic forgiveness and restitution. The phrase "*What about the bike*" has become shorthand for issues of truth in the process of seeking reconciliation.

James, a fourteen-year-old newsboy, saved his earnings for three years to finally buy the new bike of his dreams. Two days after buying the bike, Eric, the white neighborhood bully whose father was a capo of the local mob and whose uncle was the corrupt chief of police, accosted him in an alley. Eric pushed James from the bike with a "Give it up, kid!" and rode off. Powerless to do anything about the theft, James watched Eric riding his beautiful bike while he slowly returned to his rusty junker.

Three years later, Eric, having gone through his own series of tough experiences—his father's death, his uncle's imprisonment— approaches James and says:

"Uh . . . kid, could we talk?"

"I don't think so."

"Hey, come on, chill out. Just listen to me for a minute."

"I don't want to talk with you. You don't have anything to say that I want to hear."

"Yes I do, there's something I gotta say to you, OK?"

"I can't imagine what."

"Hear me out. Look, uh . . ." (Eric is stammering.) "I, uh, . . . I know I was mean to you. I, uh . . . I think about it when I see you. I uh, . . . I don't know quite how to put it. Its just that, . . . well, I uh . . . I wanted to say that I'm sorry. I apologize."

(James is incredulous.) "You . . . you are apologizing to me?" (then suspicious) "What's this all about?"

"This may sound weird, but since my dad got killed, my whole life has been turned upside down, and I've been trying to sort things out. Well, actually, I've been going to church again, and, well, I'm trying to make things right with people I hurt. So, if I hurt you in any way, I want to ask your forgiveness."

"'If you hurt me in any way,' you say?"

"Yeah. Will you forgive me?"

"Forgive you?" (long pause) "You're asking me to forgive you?"

"Yes."

"That sounds nice and all that. I mean, it may be good for you, but I have a question to ask before we talk about forgiveness."

"Yes?"

"What about the bike?"

"The bike? This isn't about the bike, it's about you and me. I don't have the bike anymore. It's long gone. Bikes? Hey, they come and they go. This is about you and me, about us, you know? About relationship."

(James breaking in) "About relationship? What relationship?"

(Eric continuing) ". . . and that's why I've come to ask, will you forgive me?"

"You think that's all there is to it? You just say 'I'm sorry' and you say some nice stuff to make everything OK again and then we forget about the past and act like nothing's happened?"

"Well . . . yes."

"I have just one thing to say."

"Yes?"

"What about the bike?"

Counseling, in whatever theory or perspective, whether the word is admissible or not permissible, fosters the practice of *forgiving*; it facilitates the search for being *forgiven*. Not all is forgivable; not all should be forgiven.

"We all have flaws, and mine is being wicked," says the Duke in *The Thirteen Clocks*, by James Thurber. Unrepentant and uninterrupted evil is not the proper subject of any discussion of forgiveness. We do not explore the moral necessity to forgive Adolf Hitler, Josef Stalin, Pol Pot, and other such for their heinous crimes against humanity. We recognize that evil is to be taken with profound seriousness, and any act of indulgence, of exculpation, is not forgiveness but easy absolution. We speak of forgiving when people turn again toward one another, when the struggle with the injury, alienation, or evil done swings from defending to reducing the distance, from increasing to decreasing the estrangement.

There is a time for forgiving and a time for recognizing that forgiveness is impossible. There are situations where reconciliation follows a breakthrough in conciliation; there are situations where it cannot and indeed should not. There are moments when forgiveness immediately follows an apology; there are times when it is necessary to ask, "*What about the bike?*"

A Bias toward Healing

The counselor who views situations of alienation or injury through a Christian frame has a bias toward healing, toward release of anger and return to open relationship. The commitment to living in loving relationship, constructive community, and continuing connection with one's fellow humans is one of the central tenets of Christian theology.

One cannot pray the Lord's Prayer from the Sermon on the Mount without facing the indivisible relationship between forgiving and being forgiven. In that same prayer we ask also for God's will to be done, and that includes those sometimes competing values of truth, integrity, and justice. A bias toward fostering forgiveness and inviting reconciliation is elemental to both practical and religious thought, while a commitment to uphold the truth, seek integrity, and pursue justice is an equally sought goal. Since each of us needs forgiveness, we who wish to be forgiven must learn the art and grace of forgiving.

Because Christian faith takes forgiving and reconciling so seriously—values it so highly—counselors must resist any attempt to minimize its difficulty, must set aside any temptation to trivialize its process, and must disavow any approach that reduces it to propositions, divine commands, common solutions, or generic answers. Since authentic forgiveness and genuine reconciliation are such crucial steps in human cooperation and community, they are essential elements of faith and life. This, however, does not prescribe the outcome or assume that each and every situation of hurt or distancing can or should be healed or bridged. Eric's pastor may have encouraged him to go to those he had injured and request forgiveness, but from James's point of view, it felt like a second attack—"You take away my bike, now you want to take away my dignity by asking me to take care of your guilt, but *what about the bike?*"

Forgiveness is both the means and end in healing interpersonal injuries. It is a means of changing perceptions, altering attitudinal set, canceling anger demands, renouncing the right to revenge, working through the obstacles to open relationship, and making contact with the offending or offended other. It is an end, as it results in reaching out to restore or renew a relationship, to be accountable for consequences, and to care about the impact one's behavior has on the other. It is a desirable option, not an expected, intended, divinely mandated outcome. It may not be the appropriate action to take or even the right alternative in many situations. Separation of combatants, cessation of abusive relationships, or distancing from toxic dynamics that are beyond a person's capacity to accept, adjust to, or absorb may be more desirable options. Forgiveness and unforgiveness, free acceptance and conditional accountability, generous pardon and firm consequences, open readmission and refusal of admission are alternatives that exist alongside one another in human community. Judgment of what is right and mercy with what falls short are both poles in the forgiving process—classically we call them judgment and grace. Christian theology takes both of these—judgment and grace—with deep seriousness. Neither can be sacrificed for easy flight into the other. However, while affirming the necessity of both, forgiveness upholds the conviction that grace has, does, and will triumph over judgment since theologically it is God's will that redemptive justice (justice that transforms both person and context in healing) will finally eclipse retributive justice (justice that repays with equal reward or logical consequence based on equivalency)—an eye for an eye.

From Trivial to Traumatic Incidents

A wide range of incidents and a spectrum of responses emerge in the counseling situation. There are *trivial incidents* in life that can be accepted with civility and tolerance. The hypersensitive counselee who takes umbrage at any perceived slight or invasion can learn the skills of offering understanding recognition of human fallibility and frailty without annoyance, irritability, or anger such as road rage. However, there are also *traumatic incidents* that scar one deeply—losses, injuries, or betrayals—that create profound narcissistic injury and serious damage to trusting relationships. The use of the word *forgiveness* to describe the healing of such profound injuries is often confusing since there is a wide range of differing definitions in both theological and psychological literature.

The following definitions occur frequently in the literature and commonly are used in the counseling interview.

(1) Forgiveness as Civility and Tolerance

Forgiveness is enlightened social tolerance, civility, and politeness that excuses an offender or an offense by offering immediate, automatic tolerance without consideration of responsibility or guilt.

This basic level of "forgiveness" is little more than memory fatigue, the exhaustion that chooses to put it behind in forgetfulness, in what is popularly called "closure." As time passes and supposedly heals all, one evicts the event, refuses to be held hostage by memory or resentment, and gets on with life.

(2) Forgiveness as Self-Liberation

Forgiveness pardons the other, not for the other's sake, or for the relationship that has been invalidated by the offense, but for one's own liberation and personal freedom.

Forgiveness is breaking free from bondage. An act of transgression locks the perpetrator to the victim; every offense creates human bondage; evil acts create chains—largely unconscious—of debt, guilt, and obligation. Forgiveness is a complex process of "unlocking" painful bondage, of individual or mutual liberation (Mueller-Fahrenholz 1997, 24).

(3) Forgiveness as Acceptance

Forgiveness accepts the other, generously and benevolently from a position of superiority, in spite of the painful actions suffered, and offers inclusion and some degree of relationship through excusing, covering, overlooking, ignoring, or denying in unselfish reframing of the event.

This level of forgiveness requires an increase in our internal motivation to repair and maintain a relationship after it has been damaged by the hurtful actions of the other (McCullough, Sandage, and Worthington 1997, 22).

(4) Forgiveness as Cohumanity

Forgiveness is the restitution of the human, the recognition of cohumanity. One human being chooses to see and accept another— in spite of a terrible past—as a fellow human being. (Yevtushenko 1967, 26, Mueller-Fahrenholz 1997)

Forgiveness that reaffirms the cohumanity of the offender is morally demanding and made possible by the offended coming to see the inherent value of all persons. It is a major step toward forgiving when one recognizes that, although the moral status of the offender may be in question, this does not diminish the person's inherent worth as a human being (Kellenberger 1995, 407).

(5) Forgiveness as Pardon

Forgiveness offers a unilateral pardon, a benevolent, generous release from all memory of and responsibility for the injury done. The character of the forgiving action arises from the one who forgives, not from the relationship or the interaction between the two.

Forgiveness is not something you do, it is something you discover—you discover you are in no position to forgive; you are more alike than unlike the one who hurt you (Patton 1990).

(6) Forgiveness as Process

Forgiveness is a process that includes both perpetrator and victim, occurring when the offender asks and the offended grants it, not unilaterally, but in an appropriate measure of mutuality.

It may be reciprocal with both sides recognizing failure, owning responsibility, moving toward each other, changing offensive behavior, releasing anger demands, healing resentments, redeeming the past, renewing the present, and opening the future to a more just relationship.

(7) Forgiveness as Contact

Forgiveness is the mutual recognition that repentance is genuine and right relationships have been restored or achieved. (Kimper, 1972)

Forgiveness is an act of recognizing remorse and repentance in the perpetrator(s) and granting the person(s) release. In repenting, one returns to the point of time (the evil act), feels the shame of victimizing or of victimization, owns the hatred, cancels the wish for revenge, and relinquishes actual and illusory power. In reciprocal repentance, both return, recognize, express remorse, and pledge change in future actions, and both release demands on the event and on the other.

(8) Forgiveness as Restitution

Forgiveness is completed by the mutual search for justice that is retributive where possible, so that the stolen is returned, the injured is cared for, and the loss is recompensed.

Where the loss is irreparable, redemptive, and transformative, justice seeks to change the relationship as well as the system around it to promote justice in the future and work for parity, mutuality, and security in both relationships and the systemic practice of fairness and respect for diversity in social solidarity.

(9) Forgiveness as Practice

Forgiveness is a habit, a practice, a craft. It is not simply an action, an emotional judgment, or a declarative utterance—though Christian forgiveness includes all of these dimensions.

Forgiveness, viewed as a practice, is a habit that must be nurtured and developed over time within the disciplines of Christian community. "Forgiveness is a habit, a practice alongside other practices including . . . confession, repentance, excommunication, prayer and healing" (Jones 1995, 163-66).

The Christian counselor recognizes that there are many different experiences of forgiving and that each injured counselee will find the way to healing arduous and demanding. The process of releasing anger, foregoing revenge, restoring positive attitude, changing behavior, and rebuilding relationship will evolve slowly in patterns not unlike the process of grieving, which it resembles. Patience with those who find it extremely difficult to let go and understanding with those who relive multiple injuries in each new insult or assault are necessary if one is to be of assistance in relational healing and the intrapersonal reconstruction of moving beyond rage and the desire for retaliation.

Visualizing the Wide Variation in Understandings

The range of definitions just cited composes a spectrum. The following chart will list definitions, the differing goals for growth, and the classic virtues that they express. Theologically, the two columns to the left are considered *neighbor love;* the third and fourth column, *enemy love;* the fifth and sixth, *forgiveness*. In a radically individualistic cultural context, such as still influences much Western psychology and theology, the words become reduced in value. Forgiveness, for the individualist, includes the first three columns; love of enemy is not commonly mentioned; and those who venture into columns four, five, and six take on heroic status claiming their fifteen minutes of fame for unexpected responses to unacceptable behavior.

A Spectrum of Constructive Responses to Injury

Civility	Acceptance	Cohumanity	Pardon	Process	Contact	Restitution
Politeness/Courtesy	Unconditional Positive Regard	Equal Regard for Other	Unilateral release	Reach out/Work through	Reconnect/Reconcile	Restore/Repay
Overlook insult or injury by refusing judgment, ignoring guilt or responsibility	Accept the other as fallible yet of worth though morally in the wrong or socially challenged in behavior	Restitution of the human; acknowledges the other as another human being in spite of hurtful acts or injurious actions	Release of demands vs. offender setting self free of review or resentment, for grieving hurt or loss	Validating repentance by one or both in mutual intention and action	Mutually recognize repentance as genuine and right relationships restored or achieved	Return to full moral community by returning what was usurped, repaying the injury
				Goals for growth in therapy		
Tolerance, openness, accepting diversity, human fallibility	Affirm self-esteem, other-regard, neighbor-love, and mutual value	Extend empathy, reciprocity, mutuality, cohumanity, compassion	Offer remission of punishment, release of revenge or retaliation	Caringly work at relating; deal with hurt/guilt/shame	Authentically risking trust, opening future, discern reality, settle for less, reward self	Justly seeking to restore the loss or repay the hurt done as possible
		Classic virtues reinforced and enhanced in the counseling process				
Civility	Grace	Mercy	Relinquishment	Agape	Shared Truth	Justice

Those counseling from a Christian frame recognize that (1) integrity of language is important in conversation about forgiving; (2) the biblical texts that inform thinking about this issue speak clearly of neighbor love (columns one and two); (3) enemy love (columns three and four) is the basis for all responses to injury; and (4) the texts on forgiveness advise conversation, contact, and restitution (columns four through seven). (See also: for neighbor, Mark 12:28-34; on enemy, Matthew 5:43-48; on forgiving, Matthew 18:15-35; Luke 17:3-6.)

With a deeply injured client, the counselor may join the denial process that is often the norm in the culture and encourage only an attitudinal shift of acceptance of the other or unilateral pardon. However, there are deeper possibilities. The offended needs the offender if healing conversation is possible; the offender needs the offended if confrontation and change is ever to happen. The columns to the left place little emphasis on truth, that is, speaking truthfully to each other and seeking to resolve differences without compromising the integrity of either party. Although this level of forgiveness appears at first glance to be an expression of mercy, in reality there is not a great deal of mercy involved. Instead, it is more a matter of denial, of overlooking the injury. It does not require much from the self or the other.

We must be aware that the goals for counseling may be set together with counselees, but it is counselees who must claim ownership, who must supply the resolve and energy to sustain the work. Growth is being done by, not for, them. Thus the outcome depends on variables within the client and between the client and what or who is significant—whether positively or negatively significant—in life and context. Knowing that forgiving is process, believing that it occurs over time and not on any imposed schedule, and recognizing that it is often dependent on variables both available and nonavailable to the counselee, the counselor must provide the gentlest of invitations and await the response.

There is a deep human need for truth to be told about an injury that cannot be denied. As counselees move toward extending mercy, they will often hesitate and freeze in fear if they must sacrifice the truth of what happened. Balancing mercy and truth in relationships tempers any application of an ideal formula that can dictate a desirable positive outcome. Mercy meets and accepts others where they are; truth asks that they come to terms with the reality of their situation. Each has the right to ask, "What about the future?" Each has the privilege of asking about the past, "*What about the bike?*"

Mercy and Truth Meet Together

Justice, argued Paul Tillich, is composed of balanced power and love—not raw power; not weak love; not coercive power; but loving power guided by powerful love. Love and power are the two pillars that support justice. Powerful love, the love that gathers all its strength to care constructively for the other, when balanced by loving power, the power that seeks the good of the neighbor, are the constituent parts of authentic justice. Powerful love is the guide; loving power the means; and the union of the two is the goal of any pursuit of justice.

These, then, can become the steps of good counseling. Further, this intertwine of love, power, and justice is especially keen when Christian counselors work with families. A parent, for example, may have the power of rank, pocketbook, and curfew over a rebellious child; but if there is not authentic love, no amount of "tough love" will ultimately prevail to rein in a child. One may win the skirmish and lose the battle. The counselor who assists parent and child to express both their needs for love and power in the relationship can begin to assist them in moving toward bridging the gap. The experience of powerful love as a guide to growth enables counselees to exercise loving power in relationships. Together, powerful love and growth can yield wisdom and effective maturity.

"Justice is composed of love and power in unity and in balance. Loveless power cannot work justice, nor can powerless love. It is powerful love and loving power that unite to produce justice" (Tillich 1954, 13). Translating this construct into the language of forgiving is theologically helpful. Mercy, the quality of love that seeks the good of the other in spite of wrongdoing, and truth, the quality of power that demands full revelation and unflinching recognition of wrong done, must be balanced in the process of seeking forgiveness. These two, mercy and truth, were the polar demands faced by the Truth and Reconciliation Commission seeking to make peace in the resolution of the atrocities of apartheid in South Africa. They are the two poles that must come together, whether in the language of theology, psychology, or philosophy. The fact that they are so often split, or the one sacrificed to the other, underscores our need for a religion that resists such reductionism. In all effective counseling, it is the union of grace and judgment that leads to growth, caring, and confrontation as they combine to support growth and adjustment.

Mercy and Truth Become One

It was the practice in Colonial New England for the community to urge a convicted criminal, sentenced to hang for his or her crimes, to repent prior to execution. If the condemned person offered an acceptable word of contrition, the community would hold a reconciliation feast in his honor and welcome him back to membership as a forgiven member of the group. Nonetheless, following the feast, they hanged him the next day (Murphy and Hampton 1988, 158). The victimizer could be valued as a person even as the value of the victim was exacted from the victimizer. Splitting truth from mercy they demanded its inevitable consequences. Mercy and truth passed each other without meeting.

Mercy, which in counseling theory is most often called *unconditional positive regard*, is the essential attitude that evokes trust and enables the counselee to risk. By definition, mercy is heartfelt compassion in the face of need, aroused in those who need not yet wish to help, but do so. Although it may be equated with kindness, grace, pity, compassion, help, forbearance, and forgiveness, it must link emotion and action or the sentiment one feels is merely sympathy. "Mercy is an *action*, or more precisely, a *reaction* to someone else's suffering, now interiorized within oneself—a reaction to suffering that has come to penetrate one's own entrails and heart" (Sobrino 1994, 16).

It is possible for persons to offer forgiveness without mercy by bestowing the "forgiving words" as a means of inflicting guilt, defending one's own moral high ground, and putting the other in his or her place as a forgiven but undeserving offender. Mercy is essential to any experience of authentic forgiveness; without it the process becomes a narcissistic exercise in self-advancement. The Christian counselor points toward mercy as the inner meaning of reaching out to the offender. Not self-liberation or personal perfection but real concern for the other motivates genuine efforts toward restoring rapport or relationship.

Truth stands as the pole of reality, of the actual occurrence, of the memory as well as the totality of the event that created injury or injustice. To deny it by rushing to resume the old way of relating, to overlook it by pretending that nothing happened, to dismiss it as though it did not truly matter, or to distort it by rewriting the story-shifting blame-spinning facts all beg the question of moral or relational injury. The truth must be faced if healing is to go deeper than emotional-bandage depth.

Kinds of Truth, Kindness in Mercy

In South Africa, the Commission for Truth and Reconciliation differentiated four kinds of legal and conclusive truth that can contribute to our discussion: (1) factual or forensic truth, based on legal and conclusive proof that is incontrovertible; (2) personal or narrative truth that is based on lived existential experience—individual or group stories and their correspondence to other accounts; (3) social or dialogue truth based on each party's attempt in dialogue to present their report or position accurately; (4) healing and restorative truth based on the common human experience of pain, loss, and encounter with evil that sees its stark reality with unblinking honesty and views it in the light of possible reconciliation.

"The latter is a different truth than the revelation of the facts. What is required is not an exact reconstruction and conclusive historical proof of what happened, but an existentially convincing testimony of the truth, both on the side of the perpetrator and the victim. Reconciliation is an act of, or on behalf of, the victims, who in freedom extend a conciliatory hand to their former enemies or oppressors" (Schreurs 2001, 138).

These are excellent steps for the counseling process, particularly where there has been abuse, injury, abandonment, or an attack on the other's integrity. The victim's truth must be told, faced, and then reexamined to find its legitimate and just place in the larger truth that embraces both sides, both stories, both experiences. The painful encounter in question must be seen in the context of the greater life narratives of the persons. In the counseling setting, the counselee tells a personal narrative truth and engages in dialogue with the counselor to seek a more accurate social truth. The movement is then toward the beginnings of a healing truth that, if extended to the offender, can become a restorative truth. Unpacking these various kinds of truth is the stuff of authentic therapy. The depth of the pain involved, layer on layer, is the raw material for profound biography. Every life is worth a novel, and in the counseling process suffering, tragedy, and loss do become literature.

Theologically, mercy and truth meet in the act of forgiving. Splitting between the two poles is inevitable when in the midst of the first pain of the offence. The counselor who continues this split within him- or herself can rarely facilitate the union of the two in the client. In the constructive union of mercy and truth, there is a restoration of perceptions of positive valuation by either or both parties. With compassion, the counselees examine the truth, and in the newly created responsibility, conversation about accountability, consequences, and authentic repentance can effectively begin. The offender can at last ask, "*What about the bike?*"

No two stories have the same plot or ending. No two marital breakdowns, for example, have identical dynamics or follow the same course in downward spiral to divorce or the slow upward climb of recovery. In each case, a renewed commitment to mercy, where trust has been violated, and truth, where honesty has been challenged, are necessary prerequisites to finding a way through the patch of bloodied emotions and perceptions.

Counseling Outcomes in Fostering Forgiving

If there is to be any possibility of forgiving or probability of not forgiving, there are questions that the counselor and counselee must ask as they review the injury. These questions, which *must* be addressed, provide a way for us to look at different end points in the forgiveness process. The questions are: Is the offender responsible or not responsible? Who is seeking release or resolution? Is the counselee requesting a return to moral community or the renewal of relationship? Is the counselee expecting to resume or restore the previous relationship or recreate or renegotiate a new relationship?

These questions can be usefully viewed in a flow pattern from nonresponsibility to renegotiation, as in the following chart.

1.
NONRESPONSIBLE?
The offender is nonculpable; the act excusable. There are extenuating circumstances. Moral criticism is not appropriate; the person is exonerated; case dismissed (i.e., it was an accident).

2.
RESPONSIBLE?
The offender is responsible; should admit culpability, own responsibility. Moral criticism is appropriate. The action is inexcusable; an actual offense was committed, must be addressed (i.e., an incident, not an accident).

3.
RELEASE?
Negative forgiveness: the offender seeks release from debt, remission of guilt or punishment, to be free (i.e., "I'm sorry, can I go?").

4.
RESOLUTION?
Positive forgiveness: the offender seeks resolution of alienation or hurt and return to an open life in community (i.e., "I'm sorry, can we go on?").

5.
REESTABLISH A MORAL COMMUNITY?
Rebuilding a moral contract, creating goodwill and respect for well-being at the level of moral community appropriate to the resolution or settlement (i.e., respect following divorce).

6.
RENEWAL OF RELATIONSHIP?
Renewal of the relationship by resuming reciprocal relating in an open future of close connections in friendship or intimacy (i.e., rekindling friendship).

7.
RESUME/RESTORE
Returning to previous, going back to the past, "the way it used to be." Resuming old life together (i.e., old, bad marriage resumed).

8.
RECREATE/RENEGOTIATE
Recreating an open, just relationship with new contract or covenant that promises a new and different future (i.e., marriage fully renewed).

Marriage counseling can provide a good example. A couple nearing a return to relationship after a serious period of separation will frequently exhibit the following pattern. The husband reports, "I just want things to be the way they used to be" (e.g., breakfast, laundry, dinner, warm bed together). This is outcome seven—resuming the old relationship. The wife will reply, "Oh no, that's what got us where we are. I want us to create a whole new way of relating" (e.g., clear communication, actual intimacy in shared life). This is outcome eight—renegotiating a new contract.

For another couple moving toward a divorce, the one may wish only to cut off the ties, end all obligations, sever the relationship (outcome three). The other spouse, thinking of the children torn between them and who will get custody, and thinking of their circles of friendship, their church, and their cotravelers from the past, insists that they return to a level playing field of joint respect and responsibility. They need a balanced mutual regard as is appropriate to persons who shared a significant period of life and who will continue to share certain responsibilities. It is a return to moral community. This is outcome five.

An injury that was clearly accidental should be accepted, as outcome one. And a nonrelated difficulty between two who do not desire a long-term relationship may be resolved in recognition of responsibility, repayment, or release, as in outcome three.

Obviously, the outcome of any movement toward healing is unique to the particular relationship; and respect for what is possible (pragmatic necessity) for the persons involved must take precedence over what may be desirable from a vision of what is healthy and wholesome (psychological dynamics) and what is morally and relationally good (theological values).

Propositions for Dialogue on Forgiveness and Reconciliation

The issues of forgiving and being forgiven are complex. It may be helpful to end with a series of propositions that seek to clarify theology and practice for the counseling situation. The following ten propositions for understanding the practice of forgiving and its relation to reconciliation summarize the perspectives that are the theological and psychological basis of the search for a practical theology of healing in relationships.

1. Accepting and forgiving are different processes.

We accept persons for the good that they are or do.

We forgive people for the evil that they did or caused.

The first is love of neighbor; the second, love of enemy.

2. Tolerating and forgiving are different processes.

We tolerate what another has done when we overlook or ignore.

We forgive what we cannot tolerate, will not overlook, dare not ignore.

When we reduce forgiving to tolerating, we choose denial instead of reality.

3. Excusing and forgiving are different processes.

We excuse people when we no longer hold them accountable.

We forgive persons when we hold them accountable but do not excuse.

When we excuse, we condone; when we forgive, we confront yet reconcile.

4. Forgetting and forgiving are different processes.

We do not need to forgive if we can simply forget—deny, detach, dismiss.

We forgive when we face injury and pain yet seek to reframe, restore, rebuild.

To equate forgiving with forgetting is to exchange healing for memory fatigue.

5. Forgiving is based on a prior step of restoring an attitude of mercy for the other.

Forgiving requires the practice of empathy that continues to see cohumanity.

When empathy breaks through one's hurt, love can penetrate the hate.

6. **Forgiving is not an arbitrary, unilateral act of mercy received as good fortune.**

Such "forgiving" bypasses the actual injury and offers no truly moral contact.

Such "forgiveness" requires no moral response to the offender.

There is a place for generous pardon; it also places the other in debt or denial.

7. **Forgiving requires a clear commitment to seek, speak, and be the truth.**

Forgiving outside of a moral universe that prizes truth is meaningless.

When we forgive we are not avoiding but addressing moral injury and injustice.

8. **Forgiving is not a moral victory for the offended that judges, controls, obligates.**

Forgiving seeks to confront, challenge, rework, and transform the relationship.

When used as a strategy for superiority, it is self-defeating and alienating.

9. **True reconciliation occurs when violence is renounced, justice sought, victims heard, innocence honored, guilt and responsibility admitted, repentance expressed, rapprochement risked, and relationship opened.**

It is costly. Both sides must open, both yield, both move, both change.

10. **Religion that is on the side of reconciliation, healing, and peace is not false. Religion that is on the side of estrangement, alienation, and destruction is not true.**

A bias toward reconciliation, a disposition toward constructive relationships, a commitment to work toward the renewal and rejoining of alienated parties, and a desire to see estranged persons or groups reconnect is essential religion (Augsburger 1996, 165-68).

CHAPTER SEVEN

Christian Counseling: Collaborating, Consulting, and Referral

When in doubt, consult.
When unclear, go for supervision.
When outside your competence, refer.
When it is better for the counselee, collaborate.

T HE MENTAL HEALTH ARENA BRINGS together persons from multiple disciplines—psychologists, psychiatrists, social workers, educators, spiritual directors, pastors, and other trained Christian counselors who serve side by side in community, are available to work cooperatively, and can welcome the unique gifts of one another's specializations. A willingness to consult, a readiness to refer, and an openness to collaborate are signs of maturity in one's profession and of integrity in one's commitment to the welfare of clients.

The Christian counselor possesses what every effective therapist longs for—a surrounding community that stands behind the counselor with understanding advocacy; a supportive community that offers a healing and empowering context to the counselee. There are settings where this is fully true and there are also churches and "churchly" culture where people see their task and calling to be something other than caring and sharing. And, to be sure, there are counselors who, having been betrayed by particular communities, try to go it alone—to their own and their clients' detriment and sorrow. Christian counselors, we maintain, understand their Christian frame begins and ends in the creation of healing community. They do this, in a large measure, by connecting and utilizing the full resources of their context—with collaboration, referral, communal support, and stimulation to be and become whole persons in the kind of community Christian scriptures call *koinonia*. This is worked out more fully in the following chapter.

A central concern of Christian ethics is the awareness of accountability and careful stewardship of privilege and opportunity. These two values shape both the professional ethics and the Christian ethics of the counselor so that a willingness to seek supervision at any point of discerned weakness or inadequacy, ensuring a commitment to stay in supervision to sustain growth, will result. Supervision is not merely a training modality or a crisis consultation; it is an ongoing expression of these ethical values of stewardship and accountability.

If a counselor argues that his or her Christian core commitments forbid reaching out for collaboration with those who differ theologically, or if religious values become a barrier to effective reliance on the resources in the community, then we raise serious concern about those core values.

The Christian counselor who is a lone ranger has at least two problems. First, totally private practice is not a responsible, trustworthy way to offer counseling. All effective counselors have immediate access to a community of colleagues, such as psychiatrists who can prescribe medication and treat; clinical psychologists who can test, diagnose, and provide therapy; and family therapists who will see the whole unit. These fellow professionals are all at their fingertips—only a phone call, an e-mail, or a shout of help away. Second, the counselor's theology is inadequate. Somewhere the false idea has lodged in the counselor's mind and will—the idea that one person can do it all without the constructive, corrective resources of community and the complementary diversity of gifts, skills, or specializations. The solitary mind of the lone therapist needs to open to collaboration; the stubborn will of the private counselor needs to soften to cooperation. We are not alone in this process of caring for the needs of persons or families. We are part of a helping community.

The counselor who tries to treat anything and everything is often less than effective at many things. We each have our strengths; we all have areas in which we are less able or proficient. Good counselors know which clients are difficult for them to reach, have issues that may fit another form of therapy more appropriately, or may exhibit deep-seated personality disorders that require specific skills, training, and expertise. The effective Christian counselor knows that all counselors have limitations. That is why building a network of fellow counselors is so important.

Effective counseling utilizes the rich skills of the surrounding community to provide needed support, additional insight, and appropriate intervention. Referral to support groups, peer counselors, twelve-step groups, or groups with special focus (such as parents of murdered children, incest survivors, sexual addiction groups—the list is long in most communities) can provide a powerful impetus to change or a source of great stabilizing strength for those who are recreating a life. Referral to fellow professionals who offer specialization extends the effectiveness of healing resources and possibilities.

When to Refer; Why One Refers

There are moments when it is clear that you should let go and help the counselee let go, so that more appropriate help is forthcoming. There are eight basic (one might say classic) reasons for making a referral to another counselor. These are (1) advanced illness requiring psychiatric intervention, institutionalization, addictions intervention, medication, and/or careful monitoring; (2) limitations to the counselor's caseload, available time, depth of training, and/or preferences in casework because of personal issues or injury; (3) puzzlement, doubts, lack of clarity about the nature of the problem; (4) the need for long-term psychotherapy that the counselor cannot provide; (5) the need for specialized agencies that are available in the community; (6) unhealthy conflict or bonding with the counselor through transference/countertransference that resist working through or resolution even with effective supervision; (7) recognition that another counselor could be of better or more immediate help; (8) assisting those who need help from another profession—for example, religious, legal, financial, or social-welfare support, educational retraining, career counseling, genetic or fertility counseling.

It is never useful to overlook or minimize those behaviors that give a clear indication of severe troubledness; for example, abrupt acute personality change, detachment and disorientation, deep depression or high elation or euphoria, commanding voices, illuminating visions, delusions of grandeur or persecution, rigid bizarre ideation, self-destructive behavior, or other indications of dissociation, inner turmoil, and loss of both center and boundaries.

When it is clear that the counselee needs special care, the counselor should have personal knowledge of the needed resources, intake policies, and the appropriate contact, which the counselor can interpret to the counselee in safe and reassuring ways. Using the relationship as a bridge that has been built over the time together, both the counselor and the counselee can take steps to cross over to the new situation of care.

The key to effective referral is clear and believable communication from the counselor that this is not withdrawal, rejection, or distancing; it is simply the two of them, reaching out to collaborative relationships that will be a great aid in this time of uncertainty and change. Further, it is crucial that the referring counselor follow through with a communication to both the client and the new counselor, that there is a follow-up confirmation that connection was made, and that support will be available if the person falters or hesitates.

It is often assumed when we speak of referral that we refer primarily to others in the field of mental health, but this is not the case. Many of the referrals made by Christian counselors are to spiritual directors, pastors, and pastoral care specialists. When the counselee approaches a significant decision in movement toward more distinct commitment to the practices of spirituality, or recognizes the need for a pivotal action in spiritual growth, the counselor may advisedly choose to commend the person to the care of a person who will function as the ongoing cotraveler in the spiritual journey, as the spiritual midwife in a rebirth, and as the representative of a Christian community. There is a therapeutic relationship that must be maintained while the person is exploring a transition from being a seeker to becoming a participant in a Christian community. The counselor may wisely choose, through referral, to collaborate in order to remain in the role and function of counselor. By encouraging another to act as priest or spiritual advisor, the counselor sustains a supportive and objective position that will prove to be crucial to personal maturation.

Counseling, Crisis Experiences, and Conversion

Counseling is a setting of safety for the client. It is a setting where it is safe to explore any issue, topic, need, interest, or potential experience that is significant to the person's life, health, and growth. It is a setting that is safe from persuasion, coercion, and imposition of any kind; it is also a place that is safe for honest confrontation, authentic encounter, and clear and clean exploration of differences, including religious convictions and commitments.

Counseling is not the context for proper conversion. It is a place for conversation about conversion, its meaning, significance, import, and impact.

Counseling is not the setting for evangelism. The therapist's role is to be an advocate for, a model of, a guide in, and a facilitator of growth in faith, but the freedom of the counselee to make important threshold decisions is protected. It is a place where conversation about issues of the client's religious experience, faith, practices, and beliefs may become important matters to be explored. The proper context for conversion is with a representative of or fellow members in the continuing community of believers that will welcome the believer into the life of shared faith and faithfulness.

Counseling is a context of caring and confrontation that bids another grow, offers the resources to enable that growth, remains available to support the person in the midst of the life decisions that they make, stubbornly stands with the person as they take the consequences for those decisions, and walks with them repeatedly through the years as they may return to do further work at crucial times in their lives.

The Christian counselor who moves between roles of therapist, spiritual director, pastor, and evangelist creates ambiguity, confuses the levels of work being done, and imposes role confusion on both the relationship and the counselee. The counseling interview may explore issues of faith commitment, examine the person's movement toward conversion, and weigh the costs and consequences of any choice or action, but the effective counselor sets clear boundaries and refers for the client's good and for the clarity of the multiple relationships involved. When a client approaches the possibility of religious conversion in the therapeutic hour, the therapist does not avoid exploration of this significant piece of work. But the therapist knows that this is an event to be experienced with a pastor or spiritual director who will become a spiritual mentor to the person and welcome them into a community of others who share this commitment.

There is a significant agenda that the counselor and counselee need to be addressing at this moment—the exploration of who serves as the counselee's pastor or director. The process of referral for renewed conversation on the meaning of this transition and experience of spiritual transformation is a significant part of the therapeutic work. The exploration of conversion's meaning, the understanding of what it offers and what it does not supply, and the recognition of the client's second thoughts all will provide future work in following sessions—work that is less likely to be done effectively if the therapist has confused the relationship by fulfilling multiple roles as counselor, advocate of a particular step, witness to commitment and covenanting, or supporter in the spiritual struggles that emerge in the integration of this new status into the previous spiritual experiences of the person.

The Many Faces of Spiritual Crisis Experiences

Conversion, for example, may be an integrative transitional experience of the redirection of life that leads to a significant advance in maturity, integrity, and constructive behavior; or it may be regressive, a return to a previous stage of development in an attempt to hold together disparate parts of a fracturing self. It may be a new integration in the present developmental stage that assists the person in fulfilling the present tasks of the particular stage, such as identity formation, intimacy achievement, generativity, fulfillment of a sense of calling and vocation, or integrity in summing up life and its meaning.

At times, a conversion may result in diffusion of ego identity, and there is no ensuing integration of the conflicted parts of the psyche, leading to increasing decomposition. If the therapist seeks to be the facilitating person in a religious crisis experience, the return to serving as a critical and objective mirror for the counselee is compromised. In contrast, when a pastor or spiritual director offers the spiritual guidance appropriate to the chosen change process, the therapist is continuously available to support, balance, question, probe, and encourage the deeper integration of new events into the personality and the person in community.

What is crucial for the counselor is authentic presence, authentic contact with the other throughout their spiritual discoveries, and authentic honesty in addressing the issues that emerge. All of these elements add up to what in Christian practice is called *authentic witness*. The therapist is a radically honest "eyewitness" to what is taking place in the client's experience of transcendence, and, as appropriate, an "I witness" to the therapist's own core commitments as an authentic human being, which can be authentically owned without imposition and authentically described without allowing those commitments to become prescribed in any way for the unique experience of the other. With this repeated use of the concept of authenticity, it is appropriate to deconstruct the idea for more explicit understandings.

The Christian Counselor and Authenticity in Witness

Authenticity comes from the Greek word *authentikos,* meaning "original"—as an authentic oil painting is an original from the actual hand of the artist. An authentic Monet is from the hand of the master; an authentic Mozart is in his musical script, or at least reproduced exactly as he composed it; authentic Chinese jade is true nephrite. To be authentic as a person is to be true to essential humanness, to be true to one's nature. Rarely is the word used in this sense in contemporary speech. Authenticity in both popular and therapeutic language has come to mean being true to one's construct of self; transparent with one's chosen motives and idiosyncratic intentions. It has come to be synonymous with "genuine" and "sincere." Important and noble as these characteristics are, they are not the core meaning of authenticity. To be authentic one would hearken back to an original, follow a model of authentic personhood, pattern life according to an exemplar of wholeness and balance, and refer to a North Star of human existence. All therapy longs for and invariably implicitly assumes, or at times asserts, is an ideal measure of humanness—of what is characteristically human. Both client and therapist need a sense of humanness that is superior to being natural, unaffected, and simply one's self. It is being a self that expresses maturity, completeness, and balance; in other words, a fully human being. Christians stake their existence on the claim that Jesus Christ is the authentic model for authentic life as an authentic person in authentic relationships and authentic community (Kraus 1979, 16).

Authentic reference can be made to this authentic model—Jesus Christ—when it is done in his own uniquely authentic way. There is no coercion, no imposition, no superior claims of an ultimate imperative that reduces the free reflection, evaluation, and final decision by the observer. The therapist who counsels from a Christian frame reports that the frame through which personhood is seen is the life, values, virtues, and relationships that are embodied in the Jesus of the Gospel documents.

The Christian counselor who seeks to embody this set of core characteristics that form the cluster of essentials we sometimes call "the Jesus Way" of relating and resolving the ongoing issues of a life does not pretend to be a neutral person. The counselor is a person with central commitments. These are not disinterested positions or perspectives, but intentional life directions, and such intentions and choices are *never* neutral. The therapist is a witness to a particular stance on life. Any witness, whether to the vision or ideas of Sigmund Freud, Carl Jung, B. F. Skinner, and so forth (the list of authorities invoked in the therapeutic process is long and varied), when offered as an idea with nothing to authenticate it, is simply a matter of words fitly spoken, full of content; perhaps appropriate to the moment's struggles, yet not a part of the actual interpersonal context. When the therapist demonstrates his or her central commitments in actions of faithful presence, concern, and service, and gives them in a manner so congruent that the content spoken and the context experienced validate each other, this "witnessed authenticity" is what Christians call embodying their faith. "Life and witness, method and message, nature and mission are one whole integrated experience" (Kraus 1979, 56).

The primary focus of such embodying of faith is not on the self, but on our common search for depth and discovery. It does not seek to change others but to offer the story of its own need for change and discovery in a way that opens dialogue. Humility and self-effacing honesty are central to the experience of Christian spirituality, and indeed essential to the spirituality of anyone doing therapy. It would be a welcome thing to see it essential to all Christian community. John Drane is pungent on this point.

> Christians love to correct other people. But an appropriate prophetic attitude for a renewed and faithful church will begin with the recognition that we can only effectively challenge others to follow the way of Christ if we are continually hearing God's voice for ourselves, and allowing our own understandings to be changed in the process. We have something to share with others not because we are different, but because we are no different, and we can become credible witnesses not as we condemn others and dismiss what we regard as their inadequate spiritualities, but as we constantly listen to the gospel and appropriate its challenge in our own lives. (Drane 2004, 99)

CHAPTER EIGHT

The Counselor as Ethicist

IN THE CLASSIC FILM SERIES *Three Approaches to Psychotherapy,* done in the 1960s, Carl Rogers is interviewing Gloria about her mother-daughter relationship when she confronts him with a question of personal morality. She reflects on her own sexual needs as a divorcée, and struggles with discussing her sexual behavior honestly with her daughter, then says, in my condensed recall of the dialogue, "I have these needs. What I would like is to be able to have sex with someone I am attracted to and not feel guilty about it. My body knows what it wants, but my conscience won't agree. That's what I want, for you to help me feel good about it." To which Rogers, the original model of client-centered nondirective counselor, now suddenly put into the position of ethicist, replies, "You want to go against your conscience and still feel good about it?" He shakes his head back and forth. "That sounds like a pretty tall order to me." ("Sorry, not possible.")

His concern as a counselor is to avoid any use of obligational or directive language—*should, ought, must*—and use words that empower the client's capacity and freedom to choose. He seeks to inform, not ask the client to conform to a code or set of rules.

He refuses to be *prescriptive* about what she "ought or ought not" to do, instead choosing to be *illuminative* about what he sees as reality. Either way he might have turned, he is, at that moment,

77

functioning as an ethicist. His commitment to authenticity as the core of personhood did not preclude the reality of her need for inner integrity.

In modern times, and even more in postmodern thought, authenticity has replaced morality. A therapeutic sensibility takes precedence over moral sensibility. The ideal self of the person counseling toward authenticity is one congruent to one's own needs, obedient to the inner directions of one's real self, and in touch with the feeling self. Morality, in contrast, points toward an ideal self that strives for integrity that requires placing limitations on the fulfillment of one's private desires when pursuing those that will endanger inner balance or infringe on the rights of others.

> In the contemporary age, authenticity is viewed as the chief "virtue" to which one should aspire. In a very limited sense, authenticity resembles the old Greek doctrine of living according to one's nature, of "knowing thyself" and "becoming what you are." But for the Greeks, one was regarded essentially as a rational being who was susceptible to moral education.... Today, by contrast ... authenticity is now pursued in the absence of any ideal about what reason or rationality requires. (Phillips 1987, 23-24)

The choice of the counselor to refuse to be prescriptive may or may not be linked to the belief in the existence of and the necessity for prescriptive morality. If the task in counseling is to facilitate the counselee in becoming a more capable and responsible self-directed person, then the preference for being illuminative will more often than not move toward that goal. In effective counseling, there are times when the counselor insistently chooses to use language that is clearly informative, declarative, or descriptive; not that which is restrictive, directive, or prescriptive. The descriptive is likely to illuminate the issues; the prescriptive to eliminate options that fall outside the imposed boundaries. At other times, the counselor may choose to use approaches that explore the restrictive, directive, and prescriptive. Counseling that explores the second of these poles is not uncommon in genetic, medical, financial, or vocational problems where expert opinion on options is desired; in intrapersonal, emotional, and relational issues it is almost exclusively the former. Each has its place and use; each can be misused. We shall explore both streams of ethical counseling theory and practice as they guide counseling from a Christian frame.

All Counseling Is Ethical Conversation

Alasdair MacIntyre argues that each culture possesses a stock of recognizable standard or "ideal characters." In Western culture, he notes, the three are the Rich Aesthete, the Manager, and the Therapist. The "character" of the therapist embodies a cultural movement that has generalized psychological technique into a sweeping program of change from virtues (what is intrinsically good) to values (what is preferentially good). "Truth has been displaced as a value and replaced by psychological effectiveness. The idioms of therapy have invaded all too successfully such spheres as those of education and religion" (MacIntyre 1984, 30-31). The therapist character is not concerned with values or ends, but with technique, "with effectiveness in transforming neurotic symptoms into directed energy, maladjusted individuals into well-adjusted ones" (MacIntyre, 1984, 30). Therapeutic values, necessary as a culturally prescribed retreat for healing and creative change, are not adequate norms for an entire culture. Subjective goodness cannot replace objective goodness without creating self-absorption and social alienation, the two besetting issues in much therapy. In the counseling room, in contrast to the cultural stereotype that is popularly disseminated, issues of morality and ethics cannot be escaped. They are present in every conversation. They may be avoided or disregarded but they are ever present.

Counseling is not a conversation that occasionally deals with questions of morality. Counseling is a conversation about morality, and counseling theory is a conversation about appropriate ethical theories. These two words, *morality* and *ethics,* often avoided in conversations about counseling and psychotherapy, are necessary, indeed essential words in describing what constitutes counseling, whether done from a Christian frame or any other chosen frame of reference. Often their use is forbidden in counselor training to inhibit the common tendency to make value judgments. The counselor must learn a variety of skills useful in protecting the client's autonomy and sustaining a "value-free" environment, and moving from a focus on moral restraints to a radical openness to deal non-judgmentally with whatever the counselee brings is a necessary practice and art. However, issues of morality do not evaporate in a value-free environment. What is right and wrong for others who are abusing the client is dealt with immediately; what is right and wrong for the client cannot be long avoided.

At the outset, several definitions of these crucial words are offered to assist in clarifying the arguments and theories that follow. Since words are frequently used imprecisely, and differences become indistinguishable, it is useful to define them again and again on the occasion of their repeated use.

> *Ethics is the study of morality; morality is the guidance of conduct.*
> *Ethics offers theories of morality; morality is the concern for right and wrong, good and evil.*
> *Ethics is the theory; morality is practice.*
> *Ethics defines how decisions should be made; morality is choosing the good, the right, the virtuous.*

The exploration of ethics is often avoided by counselors out of a concern for offering the counselee warm and supportive empathy in whatever issues they may be debating or deciding. The counselor is, by nature of contemporary Western training, committed to the classic triad of therapeutic responses—accurate empathy, nonpossessive warmth, and genuineness (Truax and Carkhuff 1967). Any thought of becoming a moral witness is equated with moralism; any consideration of ethical values and meanings is feared as being heard as judgmental.

Judgmentalism is not an unfamiliar attitude in the religious community. Its characteristics are commonly cited as: condemnation of behavior labeled as sinful; prejudging with fixed notions; inflexibility that reduces empathy and understanding; authoritarian demands for conformity; manipulating others with control that reduces their freedom; protecting others in ways that reduces autonomy; and coercion in either prohibition or direction.

Judgmentalism can reveal an ego-gratifying self-righteousness. It even contains the possibility of sadistic control. At its best it still reveals a tendency toward negativism and negation in contrast to creativity and affirmation. All of these are nontherapeutic since growth requires a significant measure of compassionate nonpossessive attention that refuses control of the other's options; an inviting openness that facilitates the articulation of real feelings; a stance against power differentials and authoritarian control; and a willingness to enhance and clarify the situation under consideration until its particularities and possibilities are fully explored without prejudging or dismissing options. Genuine support of the person and support of pursuit of the good go hand in hand.

> Without love, acceptance, forgiveness, there is no healing, no regeneration, no restoration of a broken life or a poisoned relationship. But equally, without a strong moral witness which is willing to affirm goodness and condemn evil, without the courage to risk oneself and one's relationship for moral principles, a people perish. (Hoffman 1979, 2)

The counselor who works from within a Christian frame recognizes that it is highly important to bring these two realities together, to allow them to be present in parallel ways in the counseling interview. Positive regard that affirms the counselee but avoids genuineness is incongruent. It fails to enter the moral quandary experienced by the counselee. It fails in accurate empathy. It may offer positive regard for the person but not for the development of effective and integrative behavior. Such one-sided positive regard is not the equal regard of agape. Authentic presence, prizing, and the creation of a safe context for growth require a willingness to explore what is good, right, constructive, conjoining, collaborative, and reconciling. All of these are aspects of morality in relationships and life direction.

Use of Normative Texts—Sacred Texts

When asked about offering moral guidance in the counseling process, pioneer Christian counselor and professor of pastoral counseling, and inadvertent stand-up comedian Dr. William Oglesby, at Union Theological Seminary in Richmond, Virginia, used this metaphor.

Let's imagine you have just told me of your intent to drive tomorrow from Richmond to New York. Your route, you report, is to get on Interstate 95 and drive south.

I might reply, "You are wrong. *(I am right and will set you straight.)* If you go south on I-95, you will never get to New York. *(Stupid!)* Let me draw you a map *(my infallible text)*. Do what I tell you. *(Do you get the message?)*"

(Insulted and devalued) You will want to reply, "I have maps and I know I-95 like the back of my hand. *(I am neither ignorant nor stupid.)* I do not need your advice. *(I know what I am doing)*. Besides, I did not ask you for directions. *(Get off my back)*."

I might have asked, "You are going to New York by driving south on I-95?"

"Right."

"I want to report that I have found it is 24,650 miles shorter going north on I-95."

"Really?" you say. "Actually, I've never been there. You just saved me nine months of driving."

"Yes, and it gets wet the other way, it's sometimes hard to breathe underwater, and it's cold at both poles."

By being informative rather than evaluative, or in the language of ethics, choosing to be illuminative rather than directive, the agency of the other is respected while the reality of the self is maintained. OK, you have a problem, as this book is meant to be prescriptive rather than descriptive. Might you want to reconsider and say that this book intends to be informative and illuminative?

In any discussion of ethics where there is a shared moral field of values and virtues, both counselor and counselee include tradition and text as a source of guidance in ascertaining what is good and right. How we draw on the guidance of sacred texts in ethical conversations is a crucial issue in every theory of therapy. One widely influential approach is offered by ethicist James Gustafson's contrast between seeing a sacred moral text, such as the Bible, as revealed *morality* or as revealed *reality,* as prescriptive or illuminative. The moral choice to love neighbor as self can be seen as a divinely commanded morality that one must obey whether one likes the neighbor or not. Or it can be seen as the ultimate reality of effective relationships, offering to the other what one desires for the self, living out in relationships what one has discovered is God's way with humanity and the only ultimately constructive way for humans to relate to one another.

If Scripture is the revelation of a *morality,* then its moral laws, precepts, and commands should immediately guide our decisions, literally define our options, and specifically determine our behavior. If Scripture is the revelation of *reality,* then its principles (not its laws), its central theological and ethical focus (not its particular and culturally situated precepts and commands) will guide us in discerning our decisions on contemporary issues.

Reality is defined as those theological principles that are used to interpret what "God is doing." So, we must examine what "God did" through the unfolding history of moral values, norms, and principles in the Bible and utilize these to discern what "God is doing" in the contemporary situation.

The Bible, in this latter view, becomes the background, the wide historical context, not the primary content of a moral decision; it offers the horizon of history to inform or illumine a decision process that will be faced in its present time and place, and judged on principled grounds.

The context of the therapeutic process of the twenty-first century biases the therapist toward the *illuminative.* For most counselors who seek to foster responsible agency in the counselee, talk of prescriptive moral guidance elicits an immediate reaction-formation to avoidance or silence. They recognize it is of little value to persuade the counselee, no matter how subtly it may be done, to follow the prescriptive advice of the counselor, unless that advice is to search out their own beliefs and principles and apply them consistently and responsibly. Western counseling theories permit a discussion of basic notions and values on ethics but tend to prohibit any attempt at prescribing. (This begs the question of whether the therapist should presume to be an ethical illuminator any more than a prescriber.)

In seeking to be *illuminative,* the therapist may model, facilitate, and support the development of the counselee's process of utilizing both illumination and prescription, but without taking an authoritative role as the one making the prescription. Indeed, the counselor may be an even more effective ethicist when standing alongside the counselee before the moral code in question, rather than over against, with counselor taking the side of the "moral law." In the posture of fellow seeker for redemptive truth, there is a spirit of collaboration since both are in need of virtues and values that are greater than the autonomous self.

The Moral Presumptions of the Counselor

In counseling from a Christian frame, one stands within a wide historical and a high philosophical vision of reality. The frame through which one views the world, others, and self is grounded in particular presumptions. This is not unique to any one perspective, since all counseling theories are visions of life standing on assumptive foundations; even the most rigorous scientific theory cannot exist without key agreed-upon presumptions.

Presumptions function in ethical arguments in the same way that the presumption of innocence serves in a legal argument. Innocence is assumed until adequate and demonstrated legal evidence to the contrary has been established. The burden of proof rests with the prosecution, not with the defense. In the moral sphere, we have presumptions that affirm certain foundational beliefs—both positive and negative—about human existence.

The essential presumptions that affect the practice of counseling are as follows (counseling theory will be set in counterpoint to the argument of ethicist-theologian J. Philip Wogaman [1989, 73-115]): (1) the goodness of created existence; (2) the value of the individual life; (3) the unity of the human family in God; (4) the equality of persons in God. These positive presumptions stand alongside the following negative ones: (1) human finitude limits all persons; (2) human sinfulness affects all humanity; (3) "necessary evil" is a condition or effect that frustrates the good. It is useful to express these in the language held in common by both disciplines—ethics and therapeutic counseling. Here are the four positive presumptions in terse formulation:

1. We presume the goodness of created existence. Both human creatures and the creation they inhabit have their source in a good God who intends good for humanity. To be created in the image of God; sustained by God; and loved, valued, and owned by God as prized children is good. The universe is not malevolent; the world is not evil; neither is human life and destiny; nor is the human body, its deeper dynamics, its drives, its longings, its sexuality. All are to be prized, cared for, and used wisely.

The counselee is a work of God's art, a work in progress. Together we do joint work in recovering the goodness of God's intentions for human existence. We seek together to know what is good and pursue it.

2. We presume the value and worth of the individual life. Human life is sacred. Each person is of infinite worth, not because of some individual essence, but because humanness is a supremely valuable network of related beings, related to God whom we image, and to one another, which images God to us. Faith in God is a release from frantic efforts to create some transitory illusion of value, as well as a release from callous disregard for the value of each of our fellow beings. God's immeasurable gifts—creation and grace—are prior to our response, so faith is coming to awareness, awakening from ignorance and innocence, arising from blindness to see reality with clarity.

The counselee is irreducibly valuable and will be prized as precious simply because he or she exists within the human family. We seek together to recover the sense and sensibility of worth that is grounded in the reality of our living with responsibility and reverence with others.

3. We presume the unity in God of all people and persons within the human family. Life cannot be lived in isolation. Relationship with God establishes our value as individuals and is also the basis for our unity with fellow humans, indeed, with all humanity. Authentic love is an affirmation of our basic unity in God. It is neither love seeking an object (*eros*) nor altruistic self-giving (*agape*), but mutuality in which giving and receiving are united (*koinonia*). We are corporate beings, truly human when connected, covenanted, and committed to one another in the unity of the whole human family.

The counselee is a part of a greater whole, fulfilled when united to the main, in need of connectedness to others and through others to God. We affirm together that wholeness in community is foundational to, not just consequent from, wholeness in personhood.

4. We presume the equality of persons in God. We are all equal in worth, value, and privilege. Equality is implied in the value individual persons have in their relationship to God. Persons are beyond gradation, qualification, limitation—we are beyond earthly limitation of worth because our value is based on the valuing of God who is infinite. In the ultimate perspective, one person who is totally loved by God cannot be loved less than another who is totally loved. We are equal.

The counselee is "worth-full" on the same basis as every other person. Each of us has worth, thus all are equal in value, dignity, and ultimate destiny. We struggle together to live in such respect and equality in human community.

The Moral Context of Counseling

The moral context of counseling that views clients with a Christian lens is composed of multiple and often deeply conflicting layers. The primary context is the larger social, educational, and political community that shapes our lives and values through media, educational institutions, and the social and political models that direct us. The secondary context is the faith community—the church, temple, or mosque—that was once the primary source of moral values.

The care of values and value structures is a central concern for the counselor since these are necessary to any meaningful care of the persons who live by and within those values and value systems. It is clear that the counselor shares in the task of creating, maintaining, and revising the normative value symbols of society.

> Without this more or less stable fund of normative meanings neither he [the Christian counselor] nor the secular counselor will have the luxury to bracket these meanings and concentrate primarily on dynamic and emotional issues. (Browning 1976, 98)

The counseling room is where decisions are made that affect marriage, parenting, integrity, economic responsibility, sexuality, concern for the needs of others, community solidarity, and a host of other issues from anger management and road rage to civility and coexistence with others. All these are moral issues as well as ways of coping with reality. Donald Browning makes a very insightful series of points that proceed thus:

1. Society must possess stable normative value symbols and structures. Without such a context of normative ethics, confusion arises and care becomes difficult.

2. A relatively firm and accurate moral universe that gives indices to the good and suggests appropriate actions to reach the good is necessary to foster mental health.

3. Value conflicts and value ambivalences are a major cause of problems in living and in even the more severe forms of mental illness.

4. The only way to define illness is with reference to the incapacity to fulfill the expectations that arise from a normative understanding of existence and its meaning.

5. The counselor's task is, in part, to nurture and maintain the normative values and commitments of the community. As one builds the moral community, one contributes to its health and to the health of the wider society and its members.

6. As we contribute to the moral context of our community, we strengthen the moral universe—the world of moral meanings that provides a context, a social reality for the testing of life goals and the directing of healing and growth.

Where this argument falls short is in not offering more than an ethic that focuses on finding and making the right decision (what is called a *decisionist approach*). The outlined process bases its moral choice-making on the Judeo-Christian tradition through "practical moral rationality." Although it connects this process with that of the Judaic sages, scribes, and Pharisees in pursuing a moral inquiry with integrity, it is pursuing an ethic of preferential values (what the person prefers as good), not a moral accountability in the nurturing of character and commitment (where one chooses the good because it is good). Values are things we choose because we prefer and value them; virtues are "goods" that we choose because they are good in themselves. In a later book, Browning outlines a method for practical moral reasoning. "Critical practical theologians of care" work at developing properly thought-through goals and values that will guide counseling practice.

The methodology for defining a normative practical theology of care begins with confronting a particular problem or situation in three states. First, attending to the situation and the various possible interpretations with great care (the hermeneutical process). Second, making critical analysis and comparison using the five levels of moral analysis. Third, making practical decisions about treatment.

This creates an appropriate strategy of action that embodies the norms and understandings discovered in level two (Browning 1983, 50-52).

For Browning, the five levels of practical moral reasoning are: (1) *Metaphorical level*: the basic metaphors that shape basic perceptions, beliefs, actions, and characters. (Beneath our most treasured ideas there are essential metaphors that shape our thought.) (2) *Obligational level*: the central and general principles of morality that should be seen as obligatory. (Browning believes the central ethical principle is impartiality or equal regard in contrast to utilitarianism or ethical egoism.) (3) *Tendency-need level*: the prioritizing of which tendencies and needs we are morally justified in satisfying. (This includes cultural, social, psychological, and religious understandings of which tendencies are legitimate.) (4) *Contextualpredictive level*: the interpretation of the actual situation; the context; the factors that condition it (the psychological, sociological, and cultural factors of the particular situation). (5) *Rules-roles level*: the choice of specific roles, rules, and processes of communication that we follow to accomplish our moral ends; the methods of implementation.

These levels form a hierarchy: the first is systematic theology; the second, ethics; the third through fifth, practical theology. They emerge from "a revised corelational approach." This method has a twofold source: first, from the thought of Paul Tillich, and second, Tillich's method as revised by the work of David Tracey. In Tillich's method the contemporary situation, that is, experience, can be correlated with an answer derived from revelation and the Christian tradition, that is, theology. Tracy's revision states that theology can also ask questions from experience. Hence, in the revised corelational approach, experience and theology can dialogue, each asking and each answering. This method gives more weight to the sciences and social sciences. However, this method is complex, sophisticated, time-consuming, and unwieldy for the practicing counselor. It is more attractive to academics and specialists (Pattison 1988, 45).

Decisional or Visional Ethics?

The counseling process may, in specific cases, utilize a decision-focused approach, sometimes called *juridical* or a *decisionist ethic*.

It asks such questions as, What is the problem? What are the options? What is the right thing? What ought one to do? What will you decide? The moral self of the counselee, seen as an analytic, reasoning, problem-solving agent is supported as it decides on the basis of the rules of fairness and the principles of justice that defend the right of every person to equal consideration of his or her claims in the particular situation. It seeks to assist counselees in choosing their highest values in utilizing the highest level of moral reasoning possible for the persons involved.

An alternative that is frequently more consistent with the larger therapeutic task and more inclusive of existence in community is found in visional ethics—what is called an *ethic of virtue*. It begins from the presumption that being is prior to doing; that what one ultimately chooses depends upon being a "self" that is capable of taking responsibility for choices, acts, and their consequences. *How* becomes as significant as *what* in choosing to do or not do a thing. Thus issues of ownership, integrity, and worth become central to exercising moral ability. The moral choice-maker is shaped by the continuities of selfhood we call *character*. Character is taking full ownership, centering each decision with integrity, and acting out of a deep conviction of shared worth—worth shared with significant others in community. So any idea of moral choice finds its meaning within a particular community and tradition. Each person is formed—indeed, character is formed by and constantly forms community—in distinct ways that make a free, loving, and just action a logical possibility (Hauerwas 1975, 231).

Every ethic emerges from a particular human community (secular, liberal humanist, materialistic, utilitarian, capitalist, conservative, or religious—whether Jewish, Muslim, Christian, or other). Such location situates the issue of truth and morality in the character of that community and in the character of the action in question. Each community possesses values, but is also possessed by virtues that exist above and beyond individual or group preferences. Christian ethics stands upon the basis of those virtues that are embodied in Jesus Christ. These virtues constitute the core of what is "good" in the Christian practices.

Virtues are those excellencies of character, those skills of living that enable personal, social, and societal health. Vices, in contrast, are those defects within and among us that diminish personal integration, prevent social cooperation, and divert the moral congruence of the larger society. Virtues such as hope, love, and trust are elemental human needs—basic constituents of psychological development grounded in an organic base yet requiring skill development and behavioral training.

Christian ethicist and theologian James McClendon is incisive in addressing how character is rooted in the essential developmental sequence.

> To give virtue in this way an organic base would not counter the idea that virtues require training; rather moral development might be understood as building upon the organic foundations of the life skills required for its living, much as architecture assembles materials into habitable structures. Thus particular Christian virtues could be picked out by asking what sorts of development of *homo sapiens* could best fulfill the promise implied by the open *instincts* of our species, what traits could assure the meeting of those *needs* of the embodied self that Christians can identify in themselves and in others, what skills might enhance our natural *delights* and respect our natural *horrors,* what qualities could best respect our germinal character as creatures liable to *shame, blame,* and *guilt,* and what might develop our capacity for moral *judgment.* (McClendon 1986, 104)

The practice of virtues within community provides the matrix for the development of character in community. Christian counseling is concerned about more than the alleviation of pain and discord; it is committed to the development of character that is lived out in solidarity with a community of people who share in expressing and promoting these virtues.

Virtues learned and internalized in the counseling process become the goods that define our relationships with family and society. The counselee comes to choose the virtue for its own sake, not because it works, not because it causes less pain, not because it is more socially acceptable or relationally less problematic, but because it is good and it offers its own internal rewards. In marital therapy, for example, a spouse may become aware of the virtue of *presence* and incorporate it into the practice of loving relationship by attending to the other with genuine interest, listening for the inner feelings and unexpressed longings with deepened sensitivity. If this change in behavior is motivated by the desire for payback in sexual favors or compliance with a private agenda, it will be immediately suspected by the other as manipulation, not as the virtue of loving *presence*. When love is offered as gift, the contact provides internal rewards of heightened peak experiences of intimacy that result in self-discovery as well as the surprise of the other.

Virtues, MacIntyre argues, are those practices that offer internal rewards, not the external rewards of wealth, fame, popularity, esteem, and so on. The three central virtues—truthfulness, justice, and courage—are exemplary. Truthfulness offers the internal good of trustworthiness in relationships; justice as respect of other's merits or deserts according to uniform standards will reward the inner sense of justice/fairness that is at the core of human personality; courage is the willingness to risk harm or danger to oneself out of genuine care for others and is internally rewarding as the experience of loving and being loved (MacIntyre 1984, 178-79).

If we counsel truthfully and counsel truthfulness, we are living out a virtue that offers the internal reward of trustworthiness. If we counsel fairly and counsel fairness, we are pursuing a virtue that offers the internal reward of consistency. If we counsel courageously and counsel living with courage, we are pursuing a virtue that embodies grit and guts, two incomparable goods.

In the task of counseling, truthful, trustworthy, just, equal, mutual, courageous, risk-taking, caring relationships embody therapeutic presence. They characterize the role and reality of lived morality, of experienced ethics.

When so embodied, they are illuminative.
When so practiced, they are invitational.
When so made visible, they are an invitation to collaborative Christian community.

CHAPTER NINE

Christf in
Christian Counseling

S O FAR, WE HAVE MENTIONED Jesus Christ briefly. Except
for our suggestion that proclaiming "The living Christ is with
us" be a step in the intentional model of incorporating explicitly Christian practices into counseling, much of our discussion in
this book might be interpreted as theistic, but not uniquely
Christian. That is not our intent. We believe that Christian counseling should be grounded in the peerless revelation of God seen in the
life, death, and resurrection of Jesus of Nazareth. He is the one who
is known to the eyes of faith as Jesus *the Christ*. He is that one who
faith calls "Messiah"—the one sent to be a full revelation of God's
will and way. Peter spoke for all Christians in proclaiming, "You are
the Christ, the Son of the living God" (Matthew 16:16).

Christ Is Essential for Christian Counseling

We are convinced that Christ is essential for Christian counseling.
By this, we mean that Christ's life, teaching, selfless dying, and continuing presence are the essence of constructive living, confidence
for the future, and courageous dying. Without a firm foundation in
Christ, Christian counseling is no different from religious counseling
in general—a type of counseling that has its own value, to be sure,
but that should not be labeled *Christian*. The question of this

chapter is, however, how does this assertion of the centrality of Christ specifically relate to counseling that goes by his name?

Earlier in this book, we suggested that the intentional approach should begin with the counselor saying to the client, "The Lord be with you," to which the client is encouraged to respond, "And with you, also." These statements intentionally set the stage for what transpires in the following hour of dialogue. To acknowledge the presence of God at the beginning of counseling establishes both the environment and the focus of the event. It is as if we are saying:

- God is present here; we do not meet alone.
- God has a will and way for what transpires in this session.
- Keep God in mind as we talk together.
- Never forget that God is bringing God's kingdom in through your life.
- These moments we share together are a part of holy history; we share in bringing the kingdom of our Lord into this place, this moment, and this experience.
- God has an intent for the thinking, planning, and deciding that occurs at this time and on this very day, as well as for your future from this time forth.

Any claim that begins with "God is present here" is an audacious claim.

Thus, it is not inconsequential that the counselor continues by stating, "The risen Christ is with us," and the client replies, "Thanks be to God." At this instant the context in which the counseling is to occur becomes very personal, specific, and concrete. A knowledgeable, friendly, and loving companion becomes immediately present. Jesus is a cotraveler, an example, a friend along the way.

Jesus is there. It is no longer simply a transaction between the counselor and the client(s). Another person is present. It is the risen Christ—the God who is with us is supremely revealed in Jesus, he who walked this earth and lived this life; he who knows the joys and sorrows, the success and failure, the stress and strain, the strength and weakness of being a human being, of trying to do the will of God; he who is a true life companion, who is present to stand with, reassure, encourage, direct, lift up, inspire, and forgive all the efforts the client might make to find joy and happiness.

Not only does the counselor suggest that all parties turn their attention to the presence of God, it is now proclaimed that the risen Christ is actually in the room to assist both the client(s) and the counselor in the pragmatic task of making God's will and way become functioning realities. The overall counseling goal of initiating and sustaining the presence of God in life is to be mediated through the companionship of Jesus—he who shared human life and knows what it is like to meet demands, try hard, experience failure, endue opposition, and remain faithful. He fully understands what it means to be a human being. Although we know much about the last few years of his life, for thirty years he lived the life of a carpenter in Nazareth. He empathizes completely with everyday existence. Christ is the perfect companion for those who seek help with problems. For the counselor to say, "The risen Christ is with us" is to assert this profound and basic truth.

The Christian counselor affirms that Christ is present. God is supremely revealed in Jesus. Jesus stands alongside them as they struggle with the issues of life. No matter how small or large the issue, it can receive Christ's healing touch. The ultimate goal of all counseling work is to find the way of Jesus. These moments of counseling are part of holy history. The intent is to share in bringing the kingdom of our Lord into this place, this time, this experience. When clients leave the place of counseling, they do not go out alone. Jesus goes with both the client and the counselor.

Historic Faith Applied to Counseling

These faith statements with which intentional counseling begins are but amplifications of the historic faith of the Christian tradition as it applies to counseling. In no other religious tradition is it proclaimed that the divinity had such loving concern for human beings that God sent a son to save them from their failures, their sins, and their misplaced loyalties (John 3:16). Further, in no other faith is it proclaimed that God continues to care enough to number the hairs of their heads (Matthew 10:30), treat them as his sheep (Psalm 23), and promise to never leave them (Matthew 28:20b). There is no other God like this among all the other deities of the world. Such proclamations are outrageous, amazing, outlandish, far-out, unusual, unique. They are essential and foundational to Christian faith and Christian counseling. As Paul shouted to those gathered at Mars Hill (Acts 17:22), this marvelous God, longed for but heretofore unknown, has been revealed for all to see in the person of Jesus of Nazareth, appropriately called *the Christ*. Paul spoke for all Christians when he wrote in 2 Corinthians, "God was in Christ, reconciling the world unto himself" (5:19 KJV). In Jesus we have, indeed, "put a face with the name," as the common phrase expresses it.

This last phrase about putting the face of Jesus with the name of God provokes us to say one further thing about these traditional affirmations of the Christian faith. The accusation of some has been that claiming Jesus as the Son of God implies that Christians believe in more than one God. This is not true. Although it is somewhat complicated, tradition has always contended that whereas the Son (Jesus of Nazareth) is not the same as the Father (the Creator), both are fully God. When the Holy Spirit is also included, this relationship can be illustrated in the form of a triangle that specifies the roles of Father, Son, and Holy Spirit, but also clearly indicating that each of them is fully God.

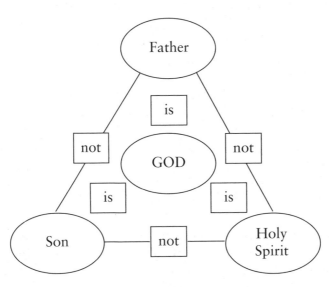

Karl Barth made the central claim of Christianity startlingly clear in his comments on the fifth chapter of Romans. He asserts that humanity's "essential and original nature is to be found, therefore, not in Adam but in Christ. . . . Adam can therefore be interpreted only in the light of Christ and not the other way around" (Barth 1956, 6). We understand what it means to be human by looking at Jesus Christ.[1] We see what it is to be human not by looking at Adam, the primate, but at Jesus, the primary example of the "ideal person." As Barth once said, "Jesus is who we are." The "new humanity," that is, Jesus, is the basis for our anthropology—our view of true humanness. This is no idle, unimportant point. One is free to choose the best or worst as exemplars when one looks to primate origins, to "nature," and assumptions from archeological digs, cultural anthropology, or historical data to define the human condition. When one looks at a person, for example, Jesus, as the paradigmatic life—an existence lived in a context recorded by witnesses from four dimensions (the Gospels) that has captured historical thought for more than two millennia—it is this understanding of humanity that commands our attention and affirmation.

The Experience of Transempirical Reality

But how can these bold affirmations about God and Christ become functional realities in the process of Christian counseling? Our answer is, "through experience." Although such a two-word answer as "through experience" might sound straightforward, the process is not self-explanatory or simple. "Through experience" requires that some psychological and philosophical reflection be added to these theological affirmations if counselors are to have the requisite understanding they need to help induce the kind of experience that they require to make these convictions become realities.

Initially, it is helpful to agree that the classic Christian affirmations we have delineated above are the kind of truths that go far beyond the empirical facts of daily life. They are sometimes referred to as "ultimate verities," "eternal truths," "supernatural convictions," "religious myths," or "faith statements." The underlying theme in all these terms is that they refer to *transempirical reality,* that is, reality that is over and beyond that which can be experienced or verified through the five senses.

Psychologists report that there is one human cognitive faculty that makes it possible for persons to experience such transempirical reality. They usually term this mental ability *imagination.* Humans can *imagine* that which they cannot see, taste, feel, hear, or touch.[2] No Christian has seen God face-to-face. Yet they are convinced of God's reality. As we noted earlier, psychologist Benjamin Beit-Hallahmi (1986) identified imagination as the common cognitive ability that can be seen in aesthetics, religion, creativity, and fantasy. Although it is problematic for some to equate their religious beliefs with artistic or musical appreciation, daydreams, and flights of fancy, the cognitive process is the same. All are grounded in imagination.

Webster's New World Dictionary (1984, 300) defines *imagination* in a helpful manner for our purposes: "(a) the act or power of forming mental images of what is not actually present; (b) the act or power of creating . . . new images or ideas by combining previous experiences; (c) the ability to understand and appreciate the imaginative creations of others." Each of these definitions is a counter to any understanding of *imagination* as "believing what you know isn't so." No one of them implies that imaginative creations are unreal or do not exist. Imaginative creations are simply perceptions of transempirical reality—a reality independent of the five senses.

It is tempting for Christians to inappropriately claim that their imaginative experience of God can be used backhandedly as proof for the empirical existence of God—a claim that may well be true but significantly exceeds human cognitive capacities.[3] We agree with Beit-Hallahmi that aesthetic appreciation is unlike religious faith in that religious faith believes it apprehends absolute truths that are truly real—even if the words that describe that reality must inevitably involve negation and analogy. This means that although humans have the capacity to experience transempirical reality through imagination, they have no words to fully describe that reality. The best they can do is to say how that reality is *like* (e.g., God is like a father; Christ is like a friend—an analogy) or *not like* (e.g., God does not change his mind; Christ did not sin—a negation) day-to-day experience (Gilke, 1959).

Inducing the Experience of God and Christ

Keeping these comments in mind, the dictionary definitions of imagination could imply the following when they are applied to the classical Christian affirmations of God's will and Christ's presence:

- Humans have the power to form mental images of God and Christ even though they can experience neither one with their five senses.
- Humans can act to use this power if they know how and desire to do so.
- Humans have the power to create images of God and Christ utilizing analogies from their daily experiences.
- Humans have the ability to understand other peoples' imaginative creations of God and Christ.
- Humans can become convinced that their imaginative creations of God and Christ are truly real and ultimately true.

The dual introits of "The Lord be with you" and "The risen Christ is with us" are meant to induce the transempirical, imaginative-creative experience we have been describing. Our experience has been that this does not automatically happen. Both counselor and counselee need to be trained in this skill even though both the counselor and counselee might be committed Christians. By invoking God's presence we are affirming our willingness and our intent to be open to God's presence and will.

We recommend the following procedures be diligently practiced: The counselor should always, and we mean *always*, spend time praying for the counselee and for guidance in the minutes just before the session begins. The client(s) should plan to arrive at least ten minutes before the session and do the following:

- With eyes closed, breathe deeply, relax, simmer down for a few minutes.
- On a pad (provided by the counselor and available with a pen in the waiting area) list the issues that she or he wants to work on during the session.

- Again, with eyes closed, silently say the two phrases that the counselor will speak ("The Lord be with you" and "The risen Christ is with us") over and over again, pausing to let the power of these words embed themselves.
- In one final prayer say, "Be with me (us), O Lord, and grant that these words spoken may become reality for me (us) in the counseling session that is come."

Of course, all human efforts are just that—"human efforts." They exist this side of heaven. There is no guarantee that an experience of God and Christ will occur but we are convinced that these experiences will never occur without intentional practice and decision. The counselor should practice a similar process, lest the opening ritual become only words.

1. Thus, according to Barth, we read the Epistles and the Fourth Gospel through the Synoptics; we read the prophets through Jesus; we read the writings and the Pentateuch through the prophets.

2. The biblical references to the experience of God confirm this contention that the experience of God is never direct. Moses heard God in a burning bush (Exodus 3:1); Samuel heard God speaking in the temple (1 Samuel 3:1); a flash of light on the Damascus Road blinded Paul (Acts 22:6), to mention only a few incidents. Among the biblical figures, only Isaiah reports seeing God face-to-face (Isaiah 6:1).

3. It is interesting to note in passing that Sigmund Freud's title for his book that disparaged religion was *The Future of an Illusion* (1957), not *The Future of a Delusion*. Freud was astute enough to know that religion was not a false idea; it was just an incorrect idea when compared to the truth of science.

Part 2

Applications

CHAPTER TEN

Conflict Mediation and Christian Counseling

IT IS OFTEN SAID THAT CONFLICT exists *within* persons as well as *between* them. This difference is easy to see. When individuals become so anxious about getting run over by cars that they will not venture out of their houses to go to work or to the grocery store, we say that they have an inner conflict. It is *within* them. When two workers become enraged with each other over what color to paint a house, we say the conflict is *between* them. It would be wise in both types of situations to seek the help of a counselor.

It is important to remember that the basic assumptions underlying Christian counseling do not change just because the situation faced by Christian counselors calls for mediation—in the one case *between* and in the other case *within* people. The ultimate goal of Christian counseling remains the same as always, namely, *to enhance and sustain the experience of God in the midst of resolving differences.* However, certain aspects of God become especially pertinent when the task at hand involves mediating so-called conflicts. The sense of God's presence in guiding, assuring, encouraging, consoling, and directing persons in their individual lives is as enduring as ever. But in mediation something more is assumed: that God has a will for resolving all human problems in a manner that accomplishes two objectives. First, the resolution fulfills the lives of the people involved at the same time that, second, it helps restore creation toward God's original intention. Jesus, the one who revealed the will of God most completely, said: "I came that they [human beings] may have life, and have it abundantly" (John 10:10). Furthermore, it was said of Jesus that "God was in Christ, reconciling the world unto himself" (2 Corinthians 5:19a KJV).

These goals of contributing to God's plan of restoration at the same time that individual lives are fulfilled may seem appropriate when the difference of opinion is a dispute over whether to give mission money to child abuse or poverty relief. But does it also apply to such a dispute as mentioned above, that is, disagreement over painting a house? The answer is yes. There is no sacred and secular distinction implied in Christian counselor mediation. In a sense both are sacred in that both are important to God. The Christian scriptures report that God commissioned Adam and Eve to "have dominion" (Genesis 1:28b).

A second question might be asked of these underlying goals of Christian mediation counseling: Do not these objectives *spiritualize* counseling in a way that ignores the reality of day-to-day practical problem solving? If by "spiritualizing" one means that resolving disputes over how to paint a house, when to discipline children, or where mission money should be spent are *not* important, then the answer is unfortunately yes. This kind of spiritualizing should be avoided in mediation. However, if by "spiritualizing" one means contextualizing the situation within a larger, transempirical reality, then the answer is no. This kind of spiritualizing should be encouraged in mediation as well as in all other counseling situations.

An illustration of a conflict between a college faculty and trustees shows the difference between these two types of spiritualizing. In a college we know of, the president formed a committee to design a long-range plan. The faculty observed that none of its members were appointed to the committee. They complained. Membership on the committee was reconsidered and two faculty members were appointed alongside four administrators and seven trustees. At the next joint trustee/faculty meeting several of the faculty loudly voiced their continued displeasure that so few faculty were included on the committee. As the meeting progressed and tempers flared, one trustee became upset over the hostile feelings. He said, "What I think we need to do is bow our heads in prayer." His request, no matter how helpful it might sound, was a way of minimizing the importance of the issue at hand—faculty representation on the long-range committee. This is not the kind of spiritualizing that Christian counselors should offer in mediation.

The question remains, What is appropriate spiritualizing? What does it mean to contextualize mediation within a transempirical reality? We think this involves several steps: It starts with reflection on the nature of conflict itself, followed by insight into the human experience of conflict, and concludes with a declaration about the ultimate foundation of self-esteem as experienced in God's action in Jesus Christ. Each of these steps is transempirical in the sense that we have stated more than once in this book. Although these processes are not meant to deny the importance of the issue over which conflict occurs, they do require stepping back from the situation and reconceiving the conflict experience within processes that are not empirically obvious. These transempirical realities can only be assumed and experienced—not observed. In the following discussion, the reader will see that these assumptions are both psychological and theological. We claim that the foundation these steps provide for conflict mediation is appropriate spirtualization.

The Nature of Conflict

The first step in appropriate or good spiritualization is reflection on the nature of conflict itself. In an earlier volume (Malony 1989), Newton Malony asserts that there is no such thing as conflict *between* people: *problems* exist *between* people; *conflict* exists *within* people. Contrary to the distinction with which this chapter began, that conflicts are of two types (*between* and *within*), all conflict of every kind is *within*. Conflict is an inner feeling, not an outer situation. Conflict is a term that is falsely applied to situations such as what color a house should be painted, where to send mission money, disciplining children, or even whether a person will be in danger if they leave home. These are *problems*, not *conflicts*. *Conflict* is a term that should only be applied to those times when a difference of opinion or internal debate is experienced as such a personal threat that persons consider taking drastic action to restore their self-esteem.

Thus, the better use of the term *conflict* is to say, "People *go into* conflict over problems." For example, if an argument over house painting becomes so drastic that workers want to get one another fired, then it would be correct to say, "The painters are *in conflict* over the painting of the house." If a mother storms out of the house and spends the night with a friend in the midst of arguing with her spouse over whether a child should be punished, it would be correct to say, "She went *into conflict* over how to discipline her child." If a member of the church's mission committee stood up and stormed out of the room, saying as he left, "I've been here fifteen years and you've never listened to my opinion. I'm leaving and I resign," then it would be correct to say, "He went *into conflict* over a dialogue about the mission budget." Conflict exists inside people, not between them.

Not all problems lead to people going into conflict. A humorous story about an older man who discovered a policeman writing a parking ticket illustrates this truth. "Can't you give an old man a break?" he asked. The policeman did not reply. "Are you deaf?" the man persisted. Still no response. The policeman put the ticket on the windshield, looked at the man, and started writing another one. "You are an insult to the police department," the old man shouted. As the policeman finished writing the fourth ticket, the old man walked away laughing. He muttered to himself, "I always like to rough up the cops. My own car is parked around the corner." What looked like a conflict was not really a conflict at all for the old man. It was not his car. His personal self-esteem was not involved. It was a problem, to be sure, but the old man did not go into conflict. Of course, the behavior of the policeman certainly indicated he was not amused at all. He kept writing tickets. Problems (defined as *differences of opinion about ways, means, or ends*) are common. *Ends* refer to the final goal (e.g., paint the house); *ways* refer to methods (e.g., paint with a brush or sprayer); *means* refer to materials (e.g., brown paint or white, oil-based or water-based paint). Problems occur every day—they can usually be typed as a ways, a means, or an end problem. Everybody has his or her own unique viewpoint. Rarely are two opinions exactly alike. When problems arise, sometimes one person quickly persuades everyone to go along with her or his point of view. More often, people have to spend time working out some resolution of their different outlooks and opinions. This is called "problem solving."

Only when solving a problem becomes personally threatening to their self-esteem do people run the danger of going into conflict. As was stated earlier, people go into conflict *over* problems. Because we live in a social world where most of our actions require interaction with other people, we are in constant danger of moving over from problems into conflict. Anxiety over whether we will get our way is very common. The graph below illustrates how often people experience the threat of going into conflict as they solve the problems of life. The graph suggests that there are three basic types of situations we all face in life:

1. **success situations** (where others support expressed personal preferences; these do not challenge us and there is no need to negotiate or compromise)

2. **stress situations** (where others challenge personal preferences and there is a need to work out some resolution of the problem and/or reach some agreements, i.e., solve problems)

3. **distress situations** (where others challenge and put down personal preferences; where we experience personal threats to our self-esteem, i.e., when persons go into conflict)

Frequency of Life Conditions

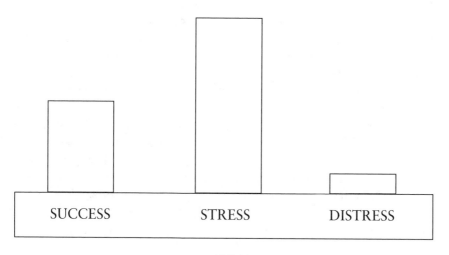

Note several things about this diagram. First, everyone has some experiences of success. These build up self-esteem and strengthen assertive personality styles. Second, everyone experiences the stress of having to solve problems. In fact, stress is normal, not abnormal. Problem solving is what people do, day in and day out. Everyday life is *stress* filled. Finally, on some occasions, everyone experiences such threats to their self-esteem that they go into conflict, or *distress*. In the average life, *distress* occurs only now and then, whereas *stress* happens almost every day. It is *distress,* or conflict, that brings people into counseling. They have taken or are afraid they will take drastic action to regain their composure, self-confidence, and/or sense of adequacy.

Why do we say that *distress,* or conflict, only happens now and then—not on a regular basis? The answer is that most of the time we solve the problems of life—we negotiate; we compromise; we bargain; we resolve our differences. Of course, our pride and self-esteem are challenged almost every time we solve problems. Things do not always go the way we plan, by any means. But enough of them do and we find enough middle ground to keep us feeling good about ourselves. But there are times when we get upset and feel truly put down and dishonored. During these periods we become distressed; we go into conflict.

Take, for example, a woman who comes to a Christian counselor because of a fight she had with her husband. She said they had been facing financial problems for some time. A month or so ago, her husband's company downsized its sales force and, although her husband was not let go, he was required to take a cut in his salary in order to retain his position. At first they looked upon the situation with the confidence that they could make it if she got a part-time job. However, she had been unable to find any work that would allow her to be at home when their young children arrived from school. As time went on, the stress of their financial problem increased. The night before she came for counseling, her husband accused her of not really trying to get a job when he discovered they would not have enough money for groceries the last ten days of the month. They had a loud argument in which she protested that she had been trying to find a job. She had gotten so upset that she accused him of wasting money on his hobby of collecting stamps.

She could not sleep most of the rest of the night. She burst out crying off and on throughout the next day. She thought of suicide. She felt hopeless. When her husband came home, they decided she should go for counseling in spite of what it might cost.

In terms of the above diagram, she went into conflict; she was distressed. Her self-esteem was so threatened that she took desperate action (the accusation about the stamp collection) to make herself feel better—that is, to restore her self-esteem. It did not work and she was so discouraged that she became depressed.

Like this woman, we know we are distressed because we want to get even, or force other people to change their opinion, or right the wrong we feel has been done to us. We feel desperate; we may feel angry, ashamed, or discounted. We may even feel helpless. We consider all the ways we can change the situation. We might even consider drastic behaviors we would not normally think we would do. Our pride has been deeply hurt and we feel misunderstood. We become discouraged and feel unloved. Sometimes, we even go for counseling, as this woman did.

Self-esteem

What is going on with us? The answer is that our self-esteem has suffered a serious threat; so much so that we may feel that we will die (psychologically or even physically) if we cannot get relief. We build up self-esteem over a lifetime of experience. There are two components of self-esteem: *role* and *reputation*. We are relational beings. We are all related inextricably to other people. That is one of the truths of the creation story in Genesis. God created Adam AND Eve—a relationship. Over the course of our lives we build up a sense of ourselves intertwined with other people. We gain our identity by who we are in the eyes of others. These are our *roles*. Roles have titles, such as father, student, computer repairman, banker, nurse, and bus driver.

As Shakespeare concluded so intuitively, life is a like a stage on which we are always playing a role with other players—both on the stage with us and in front of the audience. The psychoanalyst Erik Erickson suggested that the ego crisis of late adolescence was *role identity versus role diffusion*. Although he was thinking primarily of adolescents' need to choose a vocational role, the truth is that we are constantly playing roles in life—long before we work for wages and long after we have ceased to earn money. Our identities are tied up with the *role* (or roles) we are playing at a given time in our life; and these roles are related to the people in our lives who honor us, call us by name, support us, and provide for us the stage on which we act. They interrelate with us in the drama. They give us titles, but they also evaluate us.

These evaluations become our *reputations,* the other aspect of our self-esteem. We are constantly being judged on the basis of other peoples' opinions of how well we are doing in the roles we are playing. We have a "looking-glass self." We use others as mirrors to see who we are and, more important, how we are doing—our reputation.

Our self-esteem is the most precious thing we have; it is also the most fragile. We are persistently looking for a role to play in whatever situation we find ourselves. None of us wants to be left out. And we are constantly checking the reactions of others about how well we are playing the roles we have. The line between *stress* and *distress* in the diagram above is dotted because of this fragility—it is very easy for our roles and reputations (i.e., our self-esteem) to become threatened and for us to slip over from the stress of problem solving into the distress of going into conflict.

Both of us are professors. We teach courses. At the end of our courses students evaluate us. At the end of one course that a professor taught on adult psychotherapy, a student wrote, "This professor *needs* psychotherapy!" Wow! That was a threat to self-esteem! It was a threat to the professor's *reputation,* not his *role.* He kept his job in spite of that negative comment. In fact, when his dean heard about it, he laughed and said, "It happens to the best of us." However, when he went home that night and told his wife about the comment, she put her arms around him and said, "You are still the best in my eyes; I love you." This softened the blow. He did not go into conflict (distress). Instead, he used the student's comment to improve his teaching—that is, he problem solved. But he could have gone into conflict and sought to find out who wrote the comment and punish that student in some way. People need ways to reduce conflict and not become distressed so that they go into conflict. The professor let the laughter of his dean and the love of his wife help him maintain his self-esteem and treat the student's comment as a problem to be solved. The wife who had the violent argument with her husband over not getting a part-time job came to counseling with the hope that she could find a way to regain her self-esteem without divorce or some other drastic action.

Restoration of Self-esteem

Sister Joan Chichester, noteworthy Catholic nun who was formerly the prioress of the Carmelite Sisters nationwide, wrote in the preface to the order's book of order, "We have these rules for settling disputes in order that we will not kill each other." This may sound like an outlandish way of putting it, but there is much truth in the way Sister Joan put the matter. There can be danger that we will kill one another when we go into conflict. When we become distressed (i.e., go into conflict) we feel we are close to dying and we fight for our lives. We, like the Carmelite Sisters, need rules that will keep us from killing one another. Of course, that is what civil law is all about. Theoretically, civil law keeps us acting "civilly." To be civil means to live together and solve our problems without treating others in a way that causes them to take drastic action out of fear for their lives—their self-esteem.

What are the rules, from Christian counseling's perspective, that can be used to keep people from "killing" one another? More to the point, what can be done to help restore the self-esteem of the woman who came for counseling because of difficulty in her marriage? We would like to suggest a four-step method for conflict reduction that we believe is true to Christian affirmations and that is practical enough to work in most counseling situations. We believe that helping persons reduce their feelings of conflict (i.e., their distress) is essential to their crossing back over the dotted line and dealing with the situation at hand through problem solving. This is Christian mediation.

The four-step method for Christian conflict reduction is as follows:

Step 1. _REMEMBER:_ This is the intentional recall of the truth of Scripture that God loves us (John 3:16) and that our self-esteem is not dependent on whether our point of view wins or loses in problem solving. Such truths as that of Romans 5:8-11 overcome human forgetfulness of what God has done in God's mighty act in Jesus Christ:

> But God has shown us how much he loves us—it was while we were still sinners that Christ died for us! By his blood we are now put right with God; how much more, then, will we be saved by him from God's anger! We were God's enemies, but he made us his friends through the death of his Son. Now that we are God's friends, how much more will we be saved by Christ's life! But that is not all; we rejoice because of what God has done through our Lord Jesus Christ, who has now made us God's friends. (GNT)

Step 2. <u>REAFFIRM:</u> Step 1, *Remember,* is based on the human tendency toward forgetfulness. Even Christians who come for counseling because they are in conflict have forgotten the truths of Scripture that tell them their self-esteem comes from God who has loved them enough to send Jesus to remind them of God's love. Reading again these passages of Scripture assures that persons recall this great truth that they have forgotten. Step 2, *Reaffirm,* deals with another human problem, namely, that "saying doesn't make it so." Things we can think with our conscious minds are not always truths we experience deep down inside, that is, in our hearts.

We need to reaffirm these truths by assuring that they are experienced as really true. John Wesley, the founder of Methodism, knew the truths of the gospel many years before he experienced his heart being strangely warmed. This was reaffirmation.

Among Christians, this difficulty of making head knowledge become heart knowledge has traditionally been dealt with through prayer. As Scripture suggests, "Be still, and know that I am God" (Psalm 46:10). Prayer requires us to shut our eyes to the sights around us (i.e., the situation over which we went into conflict). Prayer then requires us to shut our mouths, quiet our minds, and experience the truth of God's love and care for us as it sweeps over our very beings. Ideally, a miracle occurs and we feel restored and self-confident. We know in our being that our ultimate self-esteem comes from God's affirmation of us as God's children. We belong to God, not to the problems we are facing.

This two-step model must not be taken as easy in every case. Most of us bring baggage to counseling that makes it hard to *remember* and *reaffirm*. Counselors will need to be very sensitive to the memories of experiences and the learned habits clients bring to counseling that might make it difficult to quickly find release by remembering and reaffirming—as profoundly true as each of these may be. Every person's selfhood is grounded in his or her unique learning history. Frequently, difficulties in the past that are only tangentially related to the current situation make sense to the client's present feeling. Counselors will need to attend to these complications and help clients become free enough from the past to acknowledge and utilize the remembering and reaffirming processes. Memories need to be healed in almost all clients who have gone into conflict.

Step 3. <u>REPENT</u>: Experiencing the self-confidence that comes from remembering and reaffirmation, persons can now reflect on the actual problem situation over which they went into conflict. Having their self-esteem made secure by the sense that God loves them just as they are, they are now able to stand back and think through the situation. For Christians, this takes the form of self-examination that leads to repentance for ways in which their behavior fell short of the will of God for those who God loves as God's children. This reflection/repentance should consider several aspects of the situation:

- Repentance for having forgotten on whose affirmation and love their true self-esteem depended; for example, Jesus' awareness that his followers would have a memory problem. He said the Eucharist should be taken "in remembrance of me" (1 Corinthians 11:23-26).
- Repentance for having thought bitter thoughts and having considered vengeful actions against others. These drastic actions against those who are also loved by God are not the will of God. Bitterness and retaliation are tantamount to thinking of others as of no value, that is, "fools," as referred to in Matthew 5:21-22. According to Jesus, this is a serious sin.
- We do not need to repent for having an opinion, taking a stand, or sharing our perceptions. God intends us, his children, to

assert ourselves. Seeing events from our point of view is acceptable. When we express our opinion we are following God's instruction to "have dominion" (Genesis 1:26). Having dominion means being good stewards of the mind God has given us. We have an obligation to become involved in what happens. So, we do not repent for having an opinion and expressing a point of view.

Step 4. <u>*REASSERT*</u>: Becoming deeply aware of God's love and care as the basic foundation for our self-esteem, and reflecting on our failure to live up to God's will in the situation, could result in our sitting back and withdrawing from the problem over which we went into conflict. But that is not the Christian way, as we noted in dealing with the question of whether *spiritualizing* would lead to thinking of real-world problems as of no importance. We concluded that God is interested in everyday reality. Problem solving that fulfills peoples' lives and advances God's restoration of God's will on earth is very important. This means that mediation in Christian counseling must lead people back into the situation in an effort to find a solution to the problem. Of course, those who have gone through steps one, two, and three are presumed to no longer be in conflict. Their self-concepts are still involved in the outcome, but their self-esteem is not threatened to the extent that they will go back into conflict. They can reenter the situation with confidence and engage in problem solving.

Admittedly, this process may seem overly optimistic. Experienced counselors know that lockstep plans rarely work as easily as they appear. Apprehending the loving support of God that leads persons back across the line from distressful loss of self-esteem to the normal stress of problem solving may come in spurts and last only for a short time for many people. It may be a slow process that will require empathic understanding from the Christian counselor. We well remember a situation involving one of us who went into conflict with another faculty member over a difference of opinion about a student. We considered taking drastic action. We refused to support motions the other person made in faculty meetings; we hoped the person would be criticized by students and even get fired; as we drove to work, we imagined what angry thing we were going to say to this person. We were *in conflict; distressed.* Suddenly it dawned on us that we were not "in charity with our neighbor," as the ritual for Holy Communion prescribed. So we sent this person a note of apology and asked for reconciliation. The person finally replied after six weeks with a note that stated, "I don't know what I can do to help you with your problem." We went back *into conflict.* We were *distressed* again. It took a month or so for us to come out of conflict enough to try reconciliation again. This story illustrates how hard it is to make the process work. Work it will, but the process may be slow; it may take time.

Conflict-free Mediation

These four steps make it possible for those who come to Christian counselors for mediation to reengage in the problem situation without being contaminated with defending and/or reclaiming their self-esteem. This is the ideal. One would hope that couples, such as the one in which the wife felt put down by her husband over not finding a job during the time of their financial crisis, would both undergo the process detailed above and be ready to work out their problems with goodwill and nondefensiveness.

However, it does not always work out that way. Often the mediator only has the chance to counsel one person in the problem situation. Sometimes being able to reduce the conflict within one person is sufficient and he or she can return to problem solving that will leave them feeling good about the resolution. At times, one person is in conflict over a problem while another person is not. Reducing the conflict in oneself can sometimes make it possible to solve a problem situation.

Nevertheless, there are predicaments that do not work out as people might hope. Problems remain. Tragedies occur. Persons lose battles. People are hurt. In these cases, there may still be success in conflict reduction for individuals themselves who undergo Christian mediation, but being "conflict free" is no guarantee that problems will be solved.

The prime example of this failure of problem resolution is Jesus himself. The whole Passion narrative (Matthew 26–28; Mark 14–16; Luke 22–24; John 18–21) reports that Jesus almost became

115

despondent and lost his self-esteem. But he remembered and reaffirmed his self-confidence in God's love and will for his life in his prayer in the Garden of Gethsemane ("not my will, but thine, be done" [Luke 22:42 KJV]) and went willingly to the cross. In a sense, the problem was not solved in spite of Jesus' reasserting himself in the situation. Jesus was crucified.

This can happen in the lives of those who receive Christian counsel. Mediation is no guarantee that things will work out to everyone's satisfaction. The possibility is there, but mediation is not always possible—if we judge success in terms of whether the problem is solved. Even in the face of the evil of failure and tragedy, Christian counseling does offer a transempirical security that will sustain those who make their faith become a reality.

Finally, such a mediation theory as we have described does not automatically dictate a method of communication or a guarantee that the theory can be put into practice. Christian counselors need to be reminded especially of the truth that counseling and preaching are different endeavors. Effective reframing of predicaments presented to them by clients is always a unique skill of its own.[1]

---

1. For a description of conflict reduction in pastoral counseling and church management, see H. Newton Malony, *Win-Win Relationships: 9 Strategies for Settling Personal Conflicts Without Waging War* (Nashville: Broadman Press, 1995).

CHAPTER ELEVEN

Counseling across Cultures

COUNSELING HAS A LONG HERITAGE. One who counsels from Christian vision and values continues a two-thousand-year-old stream of persons giving support to those in pain, offering guidance to those in a quandary, seeking reconciliation for those alienated, and fostering healing for those who are ill or injured. This long line of counselors is heir to the even longer tradition of Judaic sages who gave prophetic, priestly, and poetic shepherding to people in crisis or growth. This tradition extended to Christian counseling as it developed over time.

Although Christian counseling has developed its unique forms in hundreds of cultures throughout the centuries, and flourishes in hundreds of cultures today, *all Christian counseling, we maintain, is multicultural in origins, intercultural in content, and cross-cultural in practice.*

Christian counseling is not exclusive to any one culture. No authority can assert that what is Christian is unique to any one hemisphere, though some have claimed it so. No one ethnicity or language can dominate how to offer care to people, though many have tried, temporarily and unsuccessfully, to take control of the field and its practice. The great tree of Christian perspective has a wide-reaching network of multicultural roots. It may have a common trunk, but a profusion of intercultural branches with their own historical development, theory, and theology reach out in contrasting directions. And like the varied leaves, Christian counseling interacts with its environment with as many practices and forms as there are ethnic and linguistic people-groups who work out their Christian faith in cross-cultural conversation and dialogue. The counselor who listens to this multiform wisdom develops humility and wisdom that are necessary to any effective therapist.

The humility that is taught by learning one's multicultural history nudges the Christian counselor to shy away from dogmatic assumptions when counseling, since the knowledge of past blunders and breakthroughs made in the name of Christianity frees one to be more tentative when exploring values. The history of Christianity is a great corrective; the multiple cultures that have contributed to the development of our faith offer us a balance, a center, a permeable boundary to our theories that can open us to learn from our shared past and from the insight of all others.

The wisdom that is gained by embracing a long intercultural tradition, that is gained from standing in a river of people who have sought to bring lasting values to bear on decisions (who looked to the transcendent and universal for insight into the mundane and the particular), instructs the counselor to avoid absolute certainty about any position when counseling and opens the opportunity to be more flexible when choosing goals for living. The rich tapestry of unfolding understandings of human nature and its growth and healing can inform our counseling and transform the assumptions beneath our relating and consulting.

One Who Knows But One Culture Knows No Culture

If we are to understand culture (one who knows but one culture knows no culture), or human beings who are so richly varied (one who defines but one universal developmental pattern defines none), or to learn from the contrasts in gender (one gender taken as normative, we know, is arrogant and erroneous. Neither gender is normative for the other), or appreciate ethnicity (no group, we can be sure, is superior or inferior), or be honest about religious experience (our grasp of ultimate reality is a finite, not absolute, knowledge), or even know ourselves (we come to know who we are by being known by others), then we need other eyes. We need to see from other perspectives, standing on other ground, correcting us as they connect with us.

The therapist who expresses and embraces only the values of her parent culture, or who practices only the counseling theories of her native country or community, does not understand values, culture, therapy, or community. When one comes to know how a second culture sees "reality," one can no longer see his or her native culture in the same way again. As the French note: "What is true one side of the Pyrenees is not necessarily true on the other."

A culturally capable counselor crosses over into the counselee's culture by listening with great care, learning with a nondefensive openness, and allowing the process of counseling to be guided by how the other person is assimilating and integrating their new experiences with their cultural rootedness. However, the counselor does not become culture-free. The native culture remains the basis for the counselor's perceptions and evaluations even as they are questioned, doubted, corrected, and adjusted to come to meet the other. The counselor who claims to join a third culture, create a bridge culture, and blend the overlapping elements of both, runs the risk of losing the connection at either or both ends. To be a bridge, both ends must be grounded solidly. It is far better to cross over and be a guest in the second culture and then return illuminated by the new vision of a second take on reality.

A Cross-cultural Encounter

Consider the following case of an encounter between cultures.

A man, traveling alone in his native land, is attacked, beaten, stripped by thieves, and left for dead. Two high-status officials, both religious leaders, surprisingly offer no help. A third passerby, an alien, an outcast half-breed one would not expect to help, stops, gives aid, transports the injured man to an inn, pays for his care, and guarantees to cover costs when he returns to check on the man's recovery.

An observer interpreting the story from Western cultural assumptions might offer the following case notes: (1) visible extreme need deserves care; (2) social status is irrelevant in situations of need;

(3) crisis aid takes precedence over all other agenda; (4) common nationality or religion is no indication of willingness to help; (5) being of the same gender is no predictor of sisterly concern or fellow feeling; (6) prediction of human response in crisis is not possible; (7) absence of other persons who might pass judgment on one who ignores need makes evasion of human responsibility more likely.

Missionary anthropologist M. K. Mayers offered a sharply contrasting interpretation from his experience in a traditional Filipino culture. If this story had taken place in the location where he lived in the Philippines, he concluded, the assumptions of the traveler coming upon the wounded man might contain values such as these: (1) one feels deep compassion for anyone in need, but there are prior questions to raise before running to the rescue; (2) to find a stranger in need and offer help may place the victim under obligation and create a substantial social debt; (3) in crisis, one looks to members of his or her own family or clan for assistance, thus avoiding, as much as is possible, external obligation; (4) the first obligation of any person is to act in behalf of one's own family, not the family of another; (5) in this instance, the victim would owe the rescuer not just the costs of aid and care, but his life; (6) such a windfall would belong to the rescuer's family (family ownership versus individual ownership); (7) the first two persons passing by showed kindness and respect for the injured man by not initiating an obligation that would enslave the victim for life (Mayers 1978, 463).

Another interpretation of the scene was offered by a Filipino student in response to this story when cited in class. The preceding interpretation by Mayers, she noted, is typical of studies that use Western standards to judge the Filipino character by taking words that describe surface values and utilize them to analyze essential character and motivation. The idea of "a debt of gratitude" leading to "an obligational burden" that would interfere with offering compassionate service is confusing a surface value with a core virtue. The core virtue characteristic of the culture is "a sense of shared identity" that leads to compassionate service. Thus, (1) a sense of "fellow feeling" leads to immediate identification between the victim and the rescuer; (2) the core value of shared identity would motivate the person to act toward the other with compassion and generosity;

(3) rather than a sense of obligational burden, a warmth of gratitude will motivate the victim to seek to return the favor of aid to the rescuer or to any other person in need encountered in the future; (4) the Western interpretation, novel in its fascination with the exotic, misconstrues the dynamics of a corporate culture by interpreting it from the perspective of an individualistic culture; (5) the proper interpretation of a culture's dynamics must understand the core values and not mistake them with the surface practices of face-saving and honor maintenance. Three radically differing interpretations of the same story reveal the complexity of "crossing over" into a second culture and interpreting the picture from a foreign frame. The interpretation may be contextually congruent with cultural values held for centuries and practiced consistently by coherent communities of people, but they must be reexamined in each new situation to find their meaning in a new social location. If one is to cross over into the other worldview, it will take a special sort of empathy—perhaps more than empathy.

Seeing as Another Sees; Feeling What the Other Feels

Empathy has been variously defined, with the central element of most definitions being "entering other's" experience by hearing accurately what they say, in order to feel what they feel and, it is hoped, come to see as they see.

A common reaction to the strangeness experienced on the boundary between cultures is that the person seeking to be empathic, when puzzled by the contrasts in reactions and responses to life events, turns from empathy to sympathy. Sympathy, valuable as it is in identification with the other, is an untrustworthy process for the tasks of counseling. The metaphor of picture and frame is helpful here.

In *sympathy*, the counselor's experience is both picture and frame since the other is understood by extension of self-understanding—the observer's pain—which is identified with that of the observed. The counselor, hearing of the counselee's loss of a child, may be moved deeply by remembrance of a similar personal tragedy. In that moment, the counselor, in sympathy, may be more in touch with the memory of loss (personal frame and picture) than with the actuality of the other's grief (the picture painted by the bereaved).

In *empathy,* the counselor's experience becomes the frame, but the other's pain is the accurately perceived picture. The counselor, recalling the pain of grief (the frame), but not reliving a particular personal memory (the picture), can see the picture the other is disclosing with accuracy through the frame of empathy. In counseling that moves into a second culture, neither *sympathy,* the innate projective intuitive ability, nor *empathy,* the learned capacity to utilize imaginative projection without confusion of self and other, are sufficient. Elsewhere we have argued that the necessary ability, which must be learned and diligently cultivated, is called *interpathy.*

In *interpathy,* the other's experience becomes both frame and picture as the counselor enters a foreign culture, encounters a foreign belief based upon foreign assumptions, and chooses to share the belief, standing upon the other's assumption in order to feel the resultant feelings and their consequences in a foreign context (Augsburger 1986, 31-32).

Sympathy is a projection of one's inner feelings upon another as experiences are judged to be similar. *Empathy* is the perception of a separate other, but in practice more often fails to recognize the differing cultural assumptions, values, and patterns of thinking that encode both percepts and concepts. *Interpathy* experiences the separate other while recognizing the presence of differing assumptions, values, and views. It seeks to embrace the truly other while recognizing the difficulty, and indeed in many circumstances the impossibility, of the task, except in a partial or fragmentary way. The clarity or the caution that it produces is necessary as either a moment of wisdom or a momentary warning to go slowly, question thoughtfully, and consult diligently. The counselor brackets the familiar way of knowing—the usual epistemology—and enters another. This may require exploring notions completely foreign to one's assumed or preferred rational process that is, for the time of the encounter, suspended.

In a monocultural interpretation of the case taken from Jesus' story of the good Samaritan, a Western observer might feel sympathy for the victim, admiration for the rescuer, and disdain for the religious slackers who looked both ways, saw no one observing, and hurried by. Empathy may suggest that one man was pressed for time and rushing to an important meeting; the other, suffering from a bad back, forgot his purse; whereas the Samaritan had a means of conveyance at his disposal, financial resources, and knowledge of the nearest inn. But for the non-Filipino to enter the obligational system of a culture and sense that death by the roadside might be preferable to enslavement to an alien master in a foreign land, or that ignoring the victim may offer the opportunity for him to gather strength and save himself, or that a family search might well find him and avoid the web of indebtedness, requires a measure of *interpathy*—a change of both frame and picture.

Interpathic presence enters another world of human energies and risks, making the self available to entertain what was formerly alien and to be hospitable to what is utterly new. In *interpathy*, "feeling with" extends beyond known borders to offer respect, understanding, and grace that refuses to draw lines limiting positive regard; refuses judgments that limit coperception, so that one can join another in the other's unique world of experience. *Interpathic* listening and caring awaits the discovery of how caring is given and received in the other culture before initiating caregiving according to the patterns of one's own tradition. *Interpathic* identification prizes the meeting of humanness in which universals of life experience coincide, but it does not assume that the interpretation or the emotional savoring of these universals will overlap or necessarily even touch.

Counseling, Whether Casual or Clinical, Expresses Its Cultural Context

Whatever we say or avoid saying in a counseling encounter is shaped to some extent by the cultural context of the persons and the cultural content of their conversation. Both consciously and unconsciously, cultural assumptions shape how we see one another, what we see in one another, and what we do not see because of the instructions of our tradition to be tolerant. Cultural wisdom instructs our values and influences the choices we make in either fulfilling or negating those values in our relationships. The superficial similarities created by the dominance of Western culture may conceal the deeper differences under the blanket of shared patterns we call *westernization*. The imposition of economic dominance that reduces our global interdependence; the information explosion of media, entertainment, music-movie-print-and-video culture that provides a common language and script of popular values; the technological revolution that makes data and fantasy ever present; the militarization of both oppressor and oppressed, all tend toward the homogenization of popular culture. But this overlay does not replace the deeper levels of individual development, with its affiliations; family loyalty, with its obligations; or communal responsibilities, with their larger worldview that shapes and misshapes the formation and maturation of persons.

All counseling must be contextually congruent if it is to offer more than superficial alleviation of current difficulties. A requisite "fit" between the person and the environment must be maintained for both emotional and relational health. Counseling that alienates the person from the significant others in the counselee's life and estranges the person from the values and virtues that have been central to the formation of the personality must be carefully considered and jointly explored. Such radical change from one's embeddedness in personal-familial history requires careful evaluation and deliberate decision making, not the subtle encouragement of counseling processes.

The counselor's presuppositions about the nature of human difficulties, the balance of healthy relationships in community, the character of moral and ethical decision making, the pathways of conflict resolution, the means of reconstructing a life after crisis or loss, and the inner balance of mind and psyche in the soul all bear on the healing and growth process. None of these exist without cultural form, content, structure, and style. There are no apolitical, a-economic, amoral, a-cultural, a-philosophical, a-theological methods, techniques, theories, or practices of counseling. Every theory emerges from the values of a group—its intellectual and spiritual culture—and expresses its ethical as well as its a-esthetic presuppositions on what is "the good life."

One culture values harmony with nature, another values domination and exploitation of nature and its resources and reserves; one assumes an economy of exponential growth while another sees limits to growth as necessary; one sees our human destiny directed by fate, another by responsibility and choice. These contrasts exist both between and within cultures. Contradictory values instruct us in our living and choosing in every culture. For almost any cultural assumption held by a counselor there are equally skilled and effective therapists who question its validity or usefulness.

The wise counselor is the thoughtful counselor; thought must be given to what is reinforced by word or silence as well as what is recommended by intervention or affirmation. When a counselee is sorting out the stuff of life and its essential core commitments, the counselor who walks alongside does not trust the flow of culture and its values to go unquestioned, unexamined. A stance of suspicion is even more appropriate when reading the ingredients of a life plan than when reading the chemical composition of a breakfast cereal. If Socrates's dictum "an unexamined life is not worth living" has proved true across the millennia, then our own resolution to pursue "a life of intelligent suspicion, of informed discrimination, of principled decision" guides our way through the surrounding crosswinds of our multicultural milieu.

Counseling from a Psychology Grounded in Theology

Is the counseling from Christian commitment just expressing the views of another culture? It can be. It is less than Christian when it is. Christian faith seeks to become embedded in every culture that hosts believers, while being at the same time committed above all to a transcultural reality that is called *the reign of God*. The Christian calls this commitment to take part in God's mission in the larger human community, while living within the local and national, *serving the reign of God*. To be Christian is to be committed to working out this reign of God in all cultures, but to have as first nationality *Christian*. One can be passionately involved in a culture and at the same time give prior and ultimate allegiance to a wider humanity, to the welfare of all human beings in all cultures.

To be such a Christian one must be a dissident disciple of Jesus who refuses the powers that demand or usurp the value structures that guide life. Dissidence requires that one move beyond a secondhand "cultural" faith by insisting on firsthand "groundedness" in what one believes as a counselor. It is "groundedness" because it is the discovery of a place to stand that is one's own; although situated upon inherited cultural turf, it is more than the automatic responses programmed by ingested culture. It springs from internalized beliefs that connect one's actions and practices, modeled after a theology of God's self-giving love for humankind, to a deep love of persons, and a profound commitment to search and work for justice that is rooted in the central theme of both the Hebrew and Christian Scriptures, expressed by the Jewish prophet Habakkuk, "The just shall live by his faith" (2:4 KJV), and repeatedly cited as the central theme of internalized faith pursuing justice in life (Romans 1:17; Galatians 3:11; Hebrews 10:38; James 2:14-26). As the quotation flows from one usage to the next, each time in the four citations (that are here quoted in the sequence of the texts cited) a different word is emphasized: "The truly *just* person shall live by faith"; "It is by *faith* that the just person shall live"; "The just shall *live* by faith"; and finally, "the *just* shall *live* by *faith*" (authors' trans.). Seeking justice is faith-work; faith impels us to work for equity and equality for those we serve; living justly is faithful obedience; and all three of these elements are interdependent, indivisible, integral aspects of the Christian calling.

The counselor who is grounded in the tradition of Christian virtues possesses a referent point that is outside utilitarian values, beyond efficiency, above doing simply "what works." Discovering a center of values is a slow, demanding process. It is best done in community with other counselors, not worked out alone. Consulting, supervisory, collegial relationships are not optional if one is to build a profound faith commitment that is not simply an assent to second-hand values and belief systems. Such superficial faith is merely a continuation of a particular culture that has been assumed without the reflection, inspection, and introspection necessary if one is to be a person who facilitates growth of others.

Counseling across cultures, when done by Christians, involves not just anthropological and sociological skills; it has something that reaches down deeper, a theology that motivates reaching across barriers of misunderstanding and walls of fear and suspicion. Theology, by classic definition, is faith seeking understanding from within a cultural context. Each of the following three elements is crucial to the definition.

First, it is faith because it begins and ends with God—the One who calls us to live a just life promoting peace with one another. God is the One who transcends all cultures while being truly, absolutely related to each culture. Every culture is equidistant from God. None possesses any hegemony, has a primary access, can claim familiarity, or has any right to share in any divine superiority in relationship to any other culture. Faith in God affirms that there is a God; it is not me; not my nation, group, vision for the future, or any other human creation or possession.

Second, it is faith seeking understanding. It is attentive to all that we know of God and God's intentions for the universe and its divided and divisive citizens. It links divine and human values in ways that speak humbly of universals and stubbornly of particulars. It recognizes that we know too little of how God is drawing the world toward God's self in love, and we know too much of how we frustrate and fragment God's intentions for us to live in a more peaceful human community.

Third, it is faith seeking understanding in a *cultural context*. Christian theology, since it finds its message and method in Jesus, is always incarnational. This means it finds its authentic expression not in generalities but in specific, local, particular instances of goodness, faithfulness, and obedience to what is right and good. It risks putting on the clothes of each and every culture it enters, but without deifying that culture or sacralizing the clothes. It has a long and embarrassing history of failures in this task of embodying the way of Jesus; it has a train of moments of authenticity and truthfulness that reveals how the way of compassion and mercy can be lived out with justice and a search for what is right. It sometimes balances those two with genuine humility.

Counseling across cultures from a theological base is biased. It has a bias toward peacemaking. It has a bias toward strengthening unity between peoples without seeking to reduce the diversity. It has a bias toward increasing the dignity of each group and group member without decreasing the specialness and distinctiveness of the person or group. The Creator of diversity has presented us with a wild complementarity of peoples and cultures. Each of them is precious. None of them should be lost. Indeed, Christians look forward to a day when people of every tribe and nation and language and dialect will stand in one immense and unbroken circle around the throne of God singing a common song that will finally outsing all other songs ever sung.

Host and Guest

The metaphor for counseling across cultures that sums up the argument of this chapter is that of guest and host.

In all counseling or spiritual direction, it is the counselee who is the host, and the counselor who is the guest. This metaphor seems counterintuitive at first thought, since the counselee is calling on, entertained by, claiming time from, and taking leave from the counselor. However, it is the counselee, as host, who opens a life for the counselor's visit. It is the host, not the guest, who owns the life story that is shared in the interview. The guest is present by invitation, not intrusion, so honoring the rules of the house (cultural values) and the rules of the community (moral values) are necessary. The guest is an honorary though temporary member of the family. The house etiquette, rituals, secrets, and privacy all receive respect. The guest remains within the area assigned by the host. He or she owns only what has been brought along as necessities or received as gifts. The guest does not claim ownership of the other's story, so confidentiality is respected; the responsibility of persons for their own choices and their consequences is guarded. The guest does not overstay his or her welcome. The privilege of entering another person's private world is not taken lightly.

The boundaries, the center, the possibilities, and the pain are all the possessions of the host, not the guest. All therapy takes place on the turf of the recipient—in the life, the emotional world, and the opening future of the person desiring growth or healing. Henri Nouwen has described this relationship using the theological concept of hospitality. He counsels making room for the other, to welcome others into our lives. The host-guest metaphor reverses this paradigm. We must empty ourselves to prepare to be a guest; to be truly present in another's world; to enter it sensitively, caringly, humbly, as guests, for so we are.

CHAPTER TWELVE

Christian Counseling of Sexual Issues

THE STORY OF A FIRED KINDERGARTEN teacher at a Catholic school in Queens, New York, could easily be an example of the kind of sexual diversity situation brought to Christian counselors. She was fired for becoming pregnant out of wedlock. She informed school administrators of her condition one month after the school year began. A spokesman for the Brooklyn Catholic diocese stated that they fired her because she had violated standards stated in the personnel handbook of the school. She was devastated. "This was my first teaching job and I was looking forward to being with my young students," she exclaimed.

Of course, the church expected her to be married before becoming pregnant. She was caught in a dilemma. There was no way she could hide her condition indefinitely. The American Civil Liberties Union labeled the situation "pregnancy discrimination" and filed suit against the church.

This young woman might well seek consolation and advice from a Christian counselor who, though not a religious school administrator or perhaps not even an ordained minister, might know the teachings of many churches that state sexual relationships should occur only in marriage. Further, such a counselor might be very aware of changes in sexual mores that have made liaisons among unmarried individuals much more common. The question might be,

What is a Christian counselor to do in the face of increasing sexual diversity, religious ideals, and unintended consequences such as the situation faced by this young kindergarten teacher? Christians who counsel increasingly report these kinds of dilemmas.

Behaviors, Orientation, and Identity

One option might be for the Christian counselor to embrace these cultural changes and commiserate with those, like the young teacher, who are caught in the bind provoked by institutions, such as the Roman Catholic Church, that refuse to change with the times and embrace the new "sexual diversity." To be sure, *diversity* has come to be the *in* word these days—across a wide variety of behaviors. Typically, *diversity* is both a descriptive and a value-laden term. On the one hand, *diversity* describes, in an anecdotal manner, the array of ways in which people differ from one another, while on the other hand, *diversity* implies and advocates, in a pejorative manner, tolerance and acceptance of these differences.

Sexuality is a prime example of these two meanings of the term. Currently, diversity refers to openly acknowledged sexual behaviors that only a generation or so ago were considered culturally taboo. Sodomy, for example, has now been declared a lawfully tolerated practice of private discretion in most states where it was once considered a crime. Civil unions of gay and lesbian couples are recognized in Canada, Great Britain, and much of Europe, as well as some U.S. states. Homosexual marriage is being openly debated where it was considered anathema only a few decades ago. This increasing acceptance of diverse sexual behaviors can be seen in a recent news item regarding attorney recruitment. Under the guise of calls of justice for those who choose nonheterosexual identities (i.e., gay, lesbian, bisexual, transgendered), as a protest against the "don't ask, don't tell" rule that only heterosexuals can be members of the armed services, certain law schools have refused to allow the Defense Department to recruit attorneys on their campuses (Rooke-Ley 2005).

Much of this new acceptance of sexual diversity has come on the heels of the decisions of both the American Psychiatric Association and the American Psychological Association in the 1970s to declare homosexuality an alternative lifestyle rather than a mental illness (cf. Malony 2001). Many, but not all, associations of counselors now consider "reparative therapy," counseling designed to change sexual orientation, unethical. In the light of these changing mores, many liberal Christians (cf. Sample and DeLong 2000) now discount the value of biblical teachings prohibiting homosexual behavior as unenlightened and culture bound.[1]

The status of this dialogue on sexual diversity has much importance for Christian counselors because traditional views on these matters have tended to be less debatable and more restrictive than the current societal trend. Whereas most religious groups would agree with society's continued disapproval of pederasty, incest, adultery, and bestiality, they have also held onto such statements as "homosexual behavior is not compatible with Christian teaching." They have seen the proper role of Christian counseling to be that of helping persons overcome their inclinations to behave other than in committed heterosexual relationships. This approach has been labeled *reparative therapy* in the sense that counseling with gay, lesbian, bisexual, and transgendered persons has been directed toward "repairing" that which has gone wrong (either by nature, nurture, or sin) in the life of the individual.

This transforming or reparative therapy approach has been institutionalized into a number of counseling services such as Exodus, Desert Stream, Thomas Aquinas, and Crossover Ministries. However, since they have increasingly come to believe that sexual orientation is physiologically determined *for*, rather than chosen *by* individuals, a number of professional counseling groups have concluded that attempts to change such self-perceptions are unethical and harmful. This contrast between the teachings of their religious traditions and the assertions of other professional counselors has led to an even greater dilemma for Christian counselors. We think it is important to explore this problem further.

Two Counseling Approaches to Sexual Diversity

It is crucial to state that the difference in approaches to sexual diversity is not between good and bad basic counseling methods. In terms of adequacy, all good counseling is affirming, accepting, and nonjudgmental in basic stance. All good counseling, of whatever approach, includes two modulating, interpenetrating processes: (1) listening that builds trust and (2) advising that makes for insight and action. Further, all well thought-out counseling approaches are rhetorical in the sense that they are based on the espousal of one theory or another. However, no approach should ever be forced on persons without their permission, and every theory should be openly defined and described so that persons know the risks and benefits of the counseling they are receiving. Finally, counseling should always involve a good dose of appreciation for human frailty.

We now turn to a discussion of the foundations of contemporary social/behavioral science's approving/accepting view of sexual diversity as contrasted with Christianity's traditional transforming/reparative approach. The former view could be labeled a *social functioning model,* while the latter could be labeled an *idealistic model.* Contemporary social/behavioral science only classes behavior as pathological if it interferes with social adjustment or results in the disruption of society. All other behavior is acceptable—no matter how much tradition, culture, or prejudice may judge otherwise. Individual self-determination is affirmed and protected. "Live and let live" is the guiding maxim. Only behavior that is judged to be dangerous to oneself or others is to be labeled taboo, deviant, or insane. This kind of reasoning has permeated psychiatry and psychology for some decades. It lies behind the emptying of mental hospitals during the last quarter century, the increased tolerance for eccentricities of many kinds, and the enactment of hate crime laws to protect people from discrimination or verbal insult. Counseling is thought to be a handmaiden of these changes and owes its prime allegiance to the courts' protection of privacy and individual rights. The American Psychological Association is but one of several professional associations that have published guidelines for sexual diversity based on these principles. The underlying presumption has been that sexual identity is biologically determined—a conclusion that discounts environmental influence (Byne and Parsons 1993). Diversity has been *mainlined* and protected in the reasoning of much social/behavioral science. Thus, state boards license counselors who buy into this point of view and whom they judge will offer tolerant and permissive advice.

Conversely, *idealism* has traditionally informed the approach of the Christian faith as well as most other religions. Regardless of custom or culture, the ideal of divine intention or God's will for human life has been the basis for transforming/reparative methods. Certain actions are *pro*scribed as sinful, whereas others are *pre*scribed as those that God approves. Very often, these teachings have been counter to behaviors that were culturally acceptable at a given time. Christian ethicist Lewis Smedes stated this viewpoint thusly: "If there were no God, there would be no morality, because nothing would be intrinsically right or wrong. . . . God's design is what makes things right or wrong" (Smedes 2003, 144-45). Theologian Richard Niebuhr wrote perceptively of this tension between idealism and custom in his book *Christ and Culture* (1951). Of the several options he posed, Niebuhr discounted the tendency for religion to simply accommodate to culture. Instead, he advocated that "Christ should transform culture"—meaning that religion should always stand apart from culture and judge it in terms of a higher ideal. This is a view of life that is concerned with *norms* or *ideals,* not individuality and the social contract.

For the Christian, almost all of these idealistic or normative teachings are based on the Jewish/Christian scriptures. The Bible has much to say about sexual behavior. Fornication, adultery, homosexuality, and divorce are discouraged (1 Corinthians 6:13; Mark 10:11; Romans 1:26; Matthew 5:32), whereas marriage, fidelity, and family are affirmed (1 Corinthians 6:16; Ephesians 5:31). Of course, most of these teachings are embedded in a variety of cultural settings and, in the case of sexual behavior, it has been noted that Jesus never mentioned homosexuality. This fact has caused some to conclude that Jesus did not consider the matter of homosexual behavior to be important one way or the other.[2] Furthermore, it is claimed by some that sexual *orientation,* that is, self-understanding of one's sexual identity, was never addressed in scripture.[3]

The dilemma for Christian counselors is the fact that they are caught between the pressure to counsel out of the *idealism* of their faith or the *social functioning* of their culture.[4] The Christian counselor who chooses the social functioning approach ultimately faces the same moral dilemmas in therapy faced by the Christian counselor who chooses the idealistic approach. The *social functioning* stance provokes the counselor to deal with a series of difficult issues in the therapeutic hour. To begin the list:

- unprotected sex
- sexual promiscuity
- sadomasochism in any form
- willful infecting of a partner with a sexually transmitted disease
- absence of a sustained relationship with intimate partners

Most of these are concerns for physical health, emotional integrity, and the rejection of violence. The *idealistic* approach may vary from those who respect a lifelong commitment between lesbian partners but question any sexual activity outside the relationship, to the opposite pole of those who question any homosexual practice—either within exclusive commitment or outside of it. Thus, we argue, both approaches face the issues of boundary and proscriptions. Both prize the person and insist on individual moral agency; both seek to hold up some standard of acceptability.

The situation of the pregnant out-of-wedlock kindergarten teacher with which this chapter began is a clear example of this dilemma. Yet, in another sense, the pressure that a Christian counselor might feel in this case is no dilemma at all if one takes the story of Jesus' dealing with the imminent stoning of a woman caught in adultery (John 8:3-11) as a prime example of how Christian counselors should deal with sexual diversity. Like all Christian counselors, Jesus knew well the teaching that fornication and adultery were wrong. Yet he also knew that this was not a Sabbath meeting of the synagogue where he was the preacher of the day. The woman was about to be stoned to death. Like most counseling situations, this was a desperate moment in the life of a frail human being. It was not the time for judgment and condemnation; it was a time for mercy and empathy. After shaming those who were looking to Jesus to approve their throwing of stones, Jesus comforted the woman and sent her away with courage to change her life.

The Christian counselor begins with an unshakable commitment to the worth of persons and the importance of love and life-affirming relationships as the will of God. In counseling, the dilemma of moral and communal responsibility and the need for authentic human intimacy will not be minimized or avoided. The word *dilemma* is used, since in the situation of the exclusively attracted and oriented homosexual, there are no alternatives that do not entail sacrifice of one or the other basic convictions. The counselor stands with the client in loving authenticity while these painful alternatives are weighed, their ramifications explored, and the decision to accommodate communal values or sacrifice individual desires are painfully made. We would view with suspicion all counseling that minimizes the reality of such existential moral dilemmas or withholds loving presence from persons who are making such choices.

If we remember that the prime goal of all Christian counseling is to *enhance and sustain the experience of God in human life,* then there is no question that Jesus' interaction with the woman caught in adultery did just that. In our experience, no person ever came to Christian counselors wanting to be reminded of religion's moral teachings. They come because their lives are in disarray, their relationships are conflicted, and their feelings deeply hurt. They, like the pregnant young lady and the woman caught in adultery, were seeking understanding, support, direction, and care. They needed someone to "help them through the night," not tear them apart with judgment.

Love: The Basic Stance for Christian Counseling

Love is the single word that encompasses this approach. Christian counselors should show love to those who seek their help with problems pertaining to their sexual diversity. This love should, as we have suggested, result in persons leaving counseling with a renewed sense of God's presence—both at that moment and in the days that follow. In regard to their sexual behavior, they should expect to experience the loving presence of God in one or more of the following ways:

- The forgiveness of God if their behavior has violated God's will or has hurt another person
- The understanding of God if their behavior resulted from overwhelming pressure or their giving in to temptation
- The encouragement of God if they want to change their behavior

- The acceptance of God if they still feel tempted or have tried unsuccessfully to change their outlook
- The strength of God if they know they will be tempted to repeat behavior they feel is not the ideal
- The willingness of God to help them work out compromises that are not all good or all bad
- The trust that God will always be available and will never abandon them in their struggle to do God's will

Sexually Diverse Situations

We conclude this chapter with a list of the types of situations that might present themselves to Christian counselors.

1. A young adult is referred for counseling after exposing himself in a public bathroom.
2. A father becomes addicted to pornography.
3. A married couple feels their sex life has become stale.
4. A youth thinks she or he may be homosexual.
5. A wife or husband has been caught in adultery.
6. A professional is accused of homosexual relations with children.
7. A young unmarried woman has become pregnant.
8. A husband wants to dress in his wife's clothes.
9. A youth is caught surfing the Internet for pornographic material.
10. A married man feels he has fallen in love with a coworker.
11. A youth feels pressured to become sexually intimate.
12. A gay or lesbian couple is experiencing difficulty in their relationship.
13. A homosexual person wants to join the army.
14. A gay Christian seeks ordination in a traditional church.
15. An individual who is infected with AIDS willfully has intimate relations with another person.
16. A husband or wife feels promptings to come out of their heterosexuality and affirm their homosexuality.

This list is not exhaustive. However, it is meant to show the broad spectrum of types of situations that might be brought to a Christian counselor, where *love* is the approach to helping persons *sustain and enhance their experience of God* to help them deal with this most essential part of their lives.

1. One might question the selectivity of such deconstruction of biblical teachings such as found in Leviticus 18. Here verse 22 clearly states, "You shall not lie with a male as with a woman; it is an abomination." The validity of this verse is explained away as part of ancient Israel's "holiness code" and, thus, is not binding. It is interesting that incest (verses 7-16), adultery (verse 20), and bestiality (verse 23) are still assumed to be unacceptable.

2. There is some warrant, however, for assuming that Jesus implicitly reaffirmed the ages-old tradition that homosexuality was antithetical to the will of God and that such a conviction was so strongly affirmed that Jesus felt no need to mention it. Adultery and fornication, which Jesus does mention, were, however, still rampant during his lifetime.

3. This observation may not have a strong basis in fact since we simply do not know anything about those who engaged in homosexual behavior in Jesus' day. They could just as easily have been those with personal homosexual identity as those without it.

4. This pressure to balance faith and profession is discussed in more detail in the article "Pastoral Counseling and Sexual Identity" (Malony 2006).

CHAPTER THIRTEEN

Counseling and Family Systems

INTERESTINGLY ENOUGH, IF Newton Malony were to counsel David Augsburger (it has happened without contract or payment in the process of this collaboration), Newton would begin by inquiring about the inner conflicts that bring David to the counseling chair—cognitive, affective, behavioral, and moral conflicts that press toward resolution. By the end of the session, Newton would have a preliminary and surprisingly accurate appraisal of personality issues and interests in David's inner life.

In contrast, if David were to counsel Newton (this too has occurred), the session would begin with whatever presenting problem might be offered, but at first mention of any second party, a pencil and paper would appear and David would begin the slow sketching of the Malony genogram—the map of the family— which gradually, as the hour passed, would record two, three, or four generations of Malonys and in a preliminary way note the relational dynamics that are alive now in both conscious and unconscious issues that are being presented.

The first approach, beginning with the individual, slowly expands to include the wider family and community context. The second sees the individual in family and community as the essential unit, and begins by seeing the person living out of or living out old patterns that are both friendly and unfriendly.

Where should an authentically Christian approach to counseling focus—on the individual person, as does much Christian theology and practice, or on the person in community? Certainly there are situations where either is more appropriate. But the question mirrors a larger series of questions in counseling that begin with the basic query, Where does the problem reside?

- The problem resides in the individual—in the personality, pathology, and so forth.
- The problem is in the maternal relationship—momism, refrigerator moms, and so forth.
- The problem is in the paternal relationship—the vanishing, absent, cold father.
- The problem is in the primary triangle—the parents and the troubled child.
- The problem is in the nuclear family—-the family is the patient.
- The problem is in the multigenerational family—no symptom is only one generation deep, it usually involves three generations, with increasing impairment.

These propositions reflect the dominant perspectives of the forties, fifties, sixties, and seventies, crucial decades in theory development in the last century.

"Do you sometimes see both members of a marriage—together?" psychiatrist Nathan Ackermann reports asking of another therapist, cautiously, surreptitiously, with justified trepidation. It was the 1950s, and orthodox doctrine in classical training insisted on the individual interview as the proper setting for therapy since it was the relationship that could be expected to elicit the maximum transference from the patient. As the decades unfolded, the marriage, the parental relationships, the siblings of the troubled child (often called "the identified patient"), and eventually the three-generational tiered family became the enlarged focus of counseling. "The family is the patient," counselors began to say in shifting their primary focus from the person in open pain to the enmeshed family in denial or conflict.

Hypnotists, Puppeteers, Puppets, and More

One of the early pioneers of the family approach, the English existentialist R. D. Laing, wrote this telling metaphor of multigenerational control and manipulation:

> In the family situation, however, the hypnotists (the parents) are already hypnotized (by their parents) and are carrying out their instructions, by bringing their children up to bring their children up . . . in such a way, which includes not realizing that one is carrying out instructions: since one instruction is not to think that one is thus instructed.
>
> There are usually great resistances against this process of mapping the past onto the future coming to light, in any circumstances. If anyone in a family begins to realize he is a shadow of a puppet, he will be wise to exercise the greatest precautions as to whom he imparts this information to.
>
> It is not "normal" to realize such things. There are a number of psychiatric names, and a variety of treatments, for such realizations.
>
> Many adults (including myself) are or have been, more or less, in a hypnotic trance, induced in early infancy: we remain in this state until—when we dead awaken, as Ibsen makes one of his characters say—we shall find that we have never lived.
>
> Attempts to wake before our time are often punished, especially by those who love us most. Because they, bless them, are asleep. They think anyone who wakes up, or who, still asleep, realizes that what is taken to be real is a "dream" is going crazy. (Laing 1971, 79, 82)

The transmission of expectations, obligations, demands, invisible loyalties, and replicable patterns of behavior; the projection of myths, debts, alliances, styles of conflict, symptoms of depression, obsession, withdrawal, isolation, fusion, and enmeshment, to begin a short list of common family patterns, is an ever-present process. There are no families in which these things are not present; it is a matter of degree. Mild sharing of tendencies is the stuff of family stories and jokes; severe repetition of family pathology is the substance of tragedy. The counselor who sees individuals soon realizes that the invisible presences of family members accompany the counselee into the room and guide much that is said. The ability to see the person in a particular context is key to understanding the coherent meaning of the behavior and anxiety that it feeds on and generates for others. The insight into the interrelationship between pathology in the person and the pathological family processes that reach backward and forward allows the counselor to aid in the family's natural efforts to free itself, right itself, define itself, own and take responsibility for itself and its future, work productively, and love constructively.

The transmission of family values—central virtues that guide life choices—the overarching presence of grace and profound stubborn love and loyalty, and the willingness to work out differences and resolve old tensions in constructive ways also trickle down the family from generation to generation. Christian counselors recall the warning in the Pentateuch that the sins of the fathers are visited upon the children to the third and fourth generations that follow, but they note the promise that righteousness (read "right relationships") endures to thousands of generations. Trusting the power of love, loyalty, fidelity, and equal concern for the other's welfare to be present also in the family pattern, the Christian family therapist looks for signs of grace, rumors of goodness in each family, and seeks to nurture and support it at every opportunity.

A Bias toward Seeing Person and System Simultaneously

Counseling from a Christian frame begins from a bias that sees the individual in community as the proper unit for exploration in seeking to stimulate growth or change. The person is embedded in family, which exists within community, which is a subunit of society, which is a part of nation, hemisphere, and world. All are inextricably interrelated, interdependent, and interacting in healthy and unhealthy ways. Healthy family patterns focus on genuine balanced intimacy, affection, and collaboration between partners (the parents) that care for each other, as well as the generation that precedes and the generations that follow. They produce reasonably mature children who are relationally capable and motivated to work and serve. Unhealthy patterns are characterized by cut-off relationships, abuse, absorption, exploitation, and the denial of the above. These lead to enmeshment, victimization, and the development of pathology in person or group.

Counseling that understands the family as a living system sees the person as embodying a family's values, living out a family's rules, and expressing a family's anxiety. It sees the customary strategies of coping with stress that have been passed down from generation to generation generating troubling patterns of living. The family is composed of members who function, not independently but as an interrelated reactive or responsive whole. The parts are connected by a central sense of oneness—not necessarily friendly—that connects them voluntarily with freedom, clarity, and integrity or with either of the two extreme poles of an unhealthy "stuck-togetherness" versus an "emotional cutoff" that withdraws into distant abandonment.

Instead of surveying or introducing the various approaches that apply systems thought to the family, it is more useful to select one approach to demonstrate the power and place of family systems theory for counselors in a Christian context. From an intriguing range of theories, we will focus on the contributions of the groundbreaking theory that is foundational to virtually all that follow, the work of Murray Bowen.

Bowen family theory is coherent, well constructed, and succinct. Bowen insisted that everything he knew he had condensed to thirty pages. It is a systemic approach to seeing the family as a multigenerational organism from which members emerge at differing levels of individuation, a process he called *differentiation* (Bowen 1978). His theory, in capsule form, is a biological model of anxiety management. All persons can cope with anxiety for brief periods, but when the anxiety becomes chronic, normal safety processes fail and tension rises throughout the system. Tension overload often results in the formation of symptoms in the family, creating dysfunctions in its relationships and illness in its members. The healthy family adjusts to the tension by reducing anxiety through taking clearer positions (each is free to define self and one's own part of the relationship without need to control or define the other); less healthful families practice dominance, denial, and intrusive control strategies to convert chronic anxiety into dysfunctions, symptom formation, and illness.

In many families, anxiety is the cement that bonds them, and persons constantly scan one another for signs of tension. The ability to control the other by raising or lowering the relational anxiety is misconceived as the nature of love; Bowen once humorously commented, "A Nobel prize awaits the person who can clearly define the difference between genuine love as equal regard for the other and mutually interlocking reactive anxiety."

Families tend to function as though the individual members are absorbed, fused, involuntarily attached, like steamed sticky rice where the individual grains are stuck together into a joint ego, or a common self. As the British say, "If you've seen one member of the queen's family, you've seen them all." Or as Americans might say, "If you've seen one member of the Bush family, you've seen them all."

Bowen called this unconscious stuck-togetherness *fusion*, a neutral word to describe both *positive fusion*—dependent attachment— in which the person clings to the family ego mass in deep emotional dependence and obeys its expectations lifelong, and *negative fusion*—resistant fight or flight—in which the person tears away from the family ego fusion but continues to struggle and fight it lifelong. (No one solves a fused relationship by running away from it.) Fusion is the lack of personal maturity as an adult family member. It is the absence of personal differentiation as a self based on a delusional sense of connectedness. Differentiation is not *from* but *within* the family. It is not going one's own way from the family; it is finding one's own way within family relationships. It is a central concept that will be fully defined in the following pages. The fused person avoids taking a position on any important issue where they would have to say "I think," "I feel," or "I believe," because it would threaten the "togetherness." An "I-position" is a direct statement of belief, intention, or self-owned thought or feeling. Such statements are avoided as too risky, so the person becomes an echo, a recorded announcement, a parrot of the family's attitudes, a puppet of past generations without examining and internalizing their beliefs. When the counselee begins this movement from the immaturity Bowen calls *fusion* to authentic *differentiation* the action will affect all other parts of the family system process. To understand the family, one needs to see the interlocking series of eight relational concepts that are both descriptive of family life and prescriptive in charting a path for plotting and initiating change. These eight interlocking concepts that are universally observable in family process are:

143

1. Differentiation of Self. A person without a self shares the common self of the family "group self" or "ego mass." The goal of maturation is differentiation, or the achievement of a clearly defined and distinct self that is also able to sustain deep connections. Differentiation is not being different, distant, separated; it is being able to differ while standing together, to be distinct, not distant, separate, not separated; it balances union and separation.

2. Triangles. A family is made up of a complex network of triangles. A family of three has one triangle; a family of four has four; a family of five has ten; a family of six has twenty, and so on. In stress, two persons in relationship will triangle a third to stabilize them. A neutral third party often helps; a fused third hinders by colluding, taking sides, getting blamed, and so forth. Healthy families build strong dyadic relationships and avoid triangling against a third person.

3. Family Emotional System. There are three basic patterns of channeling anxiety. One can focus it (1) on the marriage relationship, (2) on a chosen child, or (3) on one of the partners. Families tend to project or deposit unresolved stress and this creates symptoms in a problem child, a conflicted marriage, or an ill partner. Healthy families offer each other a nonanxious presence of loving support and respect.

4. Family Projection Process. Nuclear families develop their own unique patterns of passing on the parental immaturity, tensions, and pain specifying who will be chosen, blessed, sacrificed, scapegoated, impaired, and/or absorbed. Invariably, anxiety trickles down to the weaker, or parents can set their children free by owning their own immaturity and working at their growth in open honesty.

5. Sibling Position. The rank order of persons in a family has a specific family history of meanings, a cultural set of expectations, obligations, duties, and privileges. When a child is in a parallel position with a parent of the same or other gender (the oldest child of an oldest), this may increase the weight of family demands. In healthy families, expectations are openly expressed and discussed so that each member has a part in the give and take of roles and responsibilities.

6. Emotional Cutoff. In stress, people may cut off from genuine connectedness through emotional distancing and isolation for long periods. This does not resolve the immaturity. The intensity of the cutoff and its duration through time indicate the degree of fusion and enmeshment in the family. Healthy families reconnect, restore relationships, and maintain active solidarity within, and open sharing outside, family lines.

7. **Multigenerational Process.** No symptom is one generation deep. The family process is usually visible in the family's history; severe symptoms are at least three generations deep; when cumulative, they increase in power and authority. Healthy families break old patterns by ending denial, growing in awareness of old patterns, and intentionally learning new ways of being and behaving with one another.

8. **Societal Regression or Progression.** The family is a subsystem of the surrounding community and society; it exists within and is influenced by the rise or fall, the progress or regress of communities or societies. Thus in time of war, economic depression, or natural disaster, the family may be altered by outside forces. Social change, urbanization, popular culture, education, and social mobility, as well as many other factors, can influence the family for good or ill. Healthy families adapt without losing their center and adjust to hard realities without losing one another.

To illustrate, here is a common human experience of a troubled family system. (The numbers in parentheses will identify the appropriate concept from Bowen's eight interlocking dynamics in the preceding list. As you read, refer back for comparison.)

A father is intensely attached to his two sons (3). The good first son is a conforming pleaser who seeks his father's approval (5), who conceals a spiteful brat behind his acquiescent facade, and who takes sides against his brother (2). The younger son is a rebel (5); he demands an advance on inheritance promised and then absconds with the money to a distant city, cutting off all contact (6). The older brother is outraged, blames the younger for imagined crimes, and expresses hatred (2, 5, 6).

Economic depression in the neighboring country (8) and irresponsible spending of his resources make life impossible for the younger brother (5). Having lost all his money, he decides to return home and ask for mercy and common employment at the bottom of the rung in his father's and older brother's family business (2). The father responds to the son's homecoming with typical positive attachment (1, 2, 4, 7). The older brother is outraged and refuses to join in welcoming the errant sibling (2, 5). Indeed, unlike his father, one might suspect he is more like the mother's older brother in showing symptoms of being judgmental and perfectionistic (7).

The well-known story, named for the younger son (the prodigal son), shows the power of scapegoating the one child while the more serious symptoms exist in the other. One point of the story, after all, was the older brother's unwillingness to bridge the cutoff and forgive the erring brother. When told in the original setting, it was an answer to older-brother-type critics of the Teacher's willingness to receive repentant wrongdoers.

In telling the story, Jesus is doing narrative therapy that points out the blindness and inequity of the communal system. By using the family system story as illustration, he challenges the roles of those who perceive themselves as gatekeepers (first in line) and who exclude the erring (last in line). He offers a paradigm that exposes the negative triangle and reverses its flow to lead to constructive change.

Growth and change, as seen in Bowen family theory, came from, first, recognition and awareness of the patterns that have been denied and repeated without examination. (What we deny, we most often replicate; what we resist, we repeat.) Second, change comes from owning one's own part in the family's dysfunctional process (focusing on self-stance, not other-stance or circumstance). This leads to a "pull up" in the level of differentiation or maturation and the choice of new behavior in a clear "I-position" that confronts the family with a new behavior. As the counselee identifies dysfunctional patterns, and follows the map of the genogram to recognize how these coping styles were incorporated, a new freedom to think clearly about the past, choose responsibly in the present, and live more maturely in the future is opened for consideration. The goal is not to change the family, but one's own position within it; not to reject the family, but to reconnect responsibly to it; not to flee in cutoff to the far country or to live in slavish compliance at home, but to grow to adult maturity in the coming and going of life.

Reversing the Triangles; Relating Dyadically

The power of the triangle to render the strongest person weak—in other words, the seductive power of the triangle to suck the unwitting person into collusion with a partner against a third party—is capable of making the strongest of us turn traitor to our friends for the pleasure of gossip, contempt, and presumed superiority. The invitation to talk about a person not present, to ally oneself with the person present, and to give up one's integrity and freedom is somehow almost irresistible. When one comes to understand how triangles work, how they are the primary dynamic of family fusion, how they create false alliances and phony alienations, one becomes able to not only recognize them as they are happening, but to anticipate them, predict their occurrence and plan strategies to reverse them, gently and firmly refuse them, and calmly and stubbornly stay outside them. Here are a few rules about the dysfunctions of triangles and how to behave functionally in sticky and seductive relationships. As counselors become aware of their own susceptibility to triangular dysfunctioning and take constructive steps in a personal family voyage to alter old ways of relating, they can mature in their own family relationships and simultaneously learn how to facilitate change from collusion and conspiracy (negative triangling) and move toward growth in the counselee's ways of relating in nontriangular ways to other persons both within and outside of their families.

Rule one: When two persons conflict, the most anxious person in a two-party conflict will involve a third in some way to reduce anxiety. (Adam in conflict before God says, "It was the *woman* whom *you* gave me who did this." It was *she*; it was *you*. A double triangle at first try. Genius.) A third party is brought in by one of the two to deflect or transfer the anxiety and so avoid dealing with the relationship or boundary between the two.

Rule two: When two persons get together to blame, change, fix, exclude, shame, rescue, save, criticize, or cut off a third, they create a triangle of two against one. Triangles tend to remain the same size (area) but constantly change shape. (Continuing the use of biblical stories as examples, Sarah triangles Abraham against Hagar by blaming her for letting her son abuse Sarah's son and succeeds in creating an emotional cutoff of Hagar and Ishmael. See Genesis 21:1-21.)

Rule three: When two people move close against a third, they push the third to a more distant corner. (So Sarah drives out Hagar and Ishmael and moves herself and son Isaac close to Abraham. This pushes the other two far away, without regard for their lives.)

Rule four: When two are in conflict or stress, the one will seek a third to give support in the conflict. Then the new person will "triangle" a fourth and so on and on. (This is the course of human history at war, marked occasionally by those exceptional third parties called *mediators*.)

Rule five: When the two persons agree to invite a mediator who will listen to both and help resolve the conflict with mature nontriangular principles, this creates a triad, not a triangle. A mature third party has a clear, unbiased, neutral position and seeks justice and fairness for both parties in the conflict. (A biblical example is Paul writing to Philemon to resolve the conflict between Philemon and his runaway slave, Onesimus. Or better, perhaps, as many commentators believe, Paul is teaching Philemon how to be a good third party between Onesimus and his owner Archippus. See the reference to Onesimus in Colossians 4:9, the accompanying letter, and the sudden sharp command to Archippus in 4:17 as the final word. These suggest a different reading of the little letter to Philemon.)

Rule six: When the person chooses to relate to the other one-to-one in clear dyadic honesty and refuses to carry messages, take sides, form comforting alliances, and split the world in we-they divisions (sometimes called paranoid behavior), triangles lose their power. (The Galilean, Jesus, models this most remarkably.)

Basic Guidelines to Maturity in Bowen Family Theory

There are five basic guidelines for maturing, for maintaining an "I-position" in clear differentiation of self in family and community.

1. Find a calm center within yourself; claim a clear center with others.

Find a stable balance between union with others and clear separation as a distinct human being. Maintain a firm core of solid self that is warmly connected to others yet clear in self-defined values and virtues that you prize. In Christian theology, this is being clear about self with integrity before God and being committed to work for the good of the neighbor.

2. Be nonanxious by being affirmative, not offensive.

Be clear about who you are and where you stand. Be calmly affirmative. Do not attack or accuse. Do not invade the other's feelings or thoughts. Do not attempt to control. Do not threaten or punish the other. Keep in respectful balance. This is the posture classically called "being an authentic witness to the truth," not an absolute owner, defender, or imposer of one's private truth.

3. Be nonanxious by being descriptive, not defensive.

Do not excuse or explain. Do not defend or get trapped by blame. Be in contact with your core values as well as with those of the persons you value. This willingness to give an answer without self-defense, of risking open statement of one's position without strategy or subterfuge, is confessional, vulnerable, yet most powerful.

4. Be connected to others; stay connected to others.

Do not withdraw or cut off emotionally. Do not separate relationally. Do not isolate from the other person or from your own feelings. Do not become reactive. Do not confuse distancing with growing. Do not flee from relationship. Prize, persist, and pursue loyal, faithful, loving relationships.

5. Be able to choose your responses; be a responder, not a reactor.

Do not get trapped by those who trap, hooked by those who catch and control, or irritated by those who irritate. Respond from your center, rather than reacting to theirs. Always have an emotionally neutral response that is a genuine word of respect but is not reactive. Maintain a nonanxious presence even in the midst of familial or relational anxiety processes. You are the maturing agent responsible for your life. You, ultimately, answer for who you have become, what you have made of your life.

Family dynamics can be mapped using a simple process called a *genogram*. With a family chart—showing birth order of family members and the principal patterns of projection and transmission of traits—multigenerational repetition of symptoms can be sketched during the interview, with the counselee perhaps becoming fascinated with the chart. Ten minutes into the first session, the counselee may say, "When this depression began, I felt immediate fear that I was repeating my mother and my sister's stories." The counselor takes a sheet of paper, draws the appropriate circles and lines, and with very few questions has the pattern of the nuclear family. Ten minutes later another reference to an aunt suggests adding the preceding generation. With little attention to the process of drawing a genogram, the chart has emerged from the conversation. A few closing questions and the first picture of the family dynamics has emerged. In a later session, the counselee may begin asking questions about its meaning, and further clarity will emerge. When the counselee is ready to begin bridging cutoffs, reversing triangles, reconnecting with distant members, and resolving frozen conflicts, the map will suggest directions that are appropriate.

The genogram is the Rosetta stone of family analysis. It provides a multigenerational flowchart, a map for the family voyage of discovery, a visualization of the interlocking dynamics, a schema for thinking of ambivalent relationships, an eye-opening means of dispelling the fog of denial, and an unforgettable sketch of many forgotten facets of family health and pathology. It is not an exercise in genealogy, although it utilizes many of the same bits of data. It is a relational chart that identifies the qualities of union and separation in all interpersonal experiences with those "who love us most."

Treating the family is far more powerful in eliciting change because the change comes from within the family itself. If the family has the power to bind and control, intimidate and obligate (and we know it does), that same power can be used to free and respect, liberate and emancipate its members. The power to change lies not in the counselor, but in the family. As denial is dispelled, the invisible are made visible, the silent find a voice, the powerless claim unused power, and the alienated return home.

Part 3

Destiny

CHAPTER FOURTEEN

Christian Counseling in the Postmodern World

W E HAVE TOUTED THE NEW atmosphere created by postmodernism more than once in this volume. This may sound strange to those who thought that we were reveling in an environment where everything was relative and where no one could claim anything was absolutely true anymore. This kind of reaction is understandable. However, we are convinced that a postmodern outlook does, indeed, provide a place for Christian counseling that it has not enjoyed heretofore.

Modernism

It is important to be clear about what is meant by *modernism* if this contention that *postmodernism* is supportive of Christian counseling is to make sense. Although it is often said that the presumptions underlying modernism began with the Enlightenment of the eighteenth century, a clear representative of these ideals in the twentieth century was the 1927 publication of Sigmund Freud's *Future of an Illusion*. Freud espoused the view that religion was an "illusion" that had no future—a point of view that had been germinating since the sixteenth-century skeptical humanism of Erasmus and the scientific revolution of Galileo. Freud advocated a reliance on rational thought and scientific empiricism in contrast to what he termed the "neurotic wish fulfillment" basis of Western religion. Freud would be amazed that religion survived the twentieth-century onslaught of science and technology. He died in 1939. However, some have contended that had Freud lived until later in the twentieth century he would have changed his denigrating attitude toward religion.

In some sense, it is amazing that religion survived in a century where modernism truly came of age. The objective truth of science has overwhelmed the revealed authority of religion. At best, religious truth has been strictly relegated to the irrationality of emotions and moralisms. In psychology, for example, religion became a taboo topic (cf. Beit-Hallahmi 1977) that was relegated to the realm of superstition and abnormality. At midcentury, religion received a slight boost in reputation with the publication of Gordon Allport's *Individual and His Religion: A Psychological Interpretation* (1950) and Walter Houston Clark's *Psychology of Religion: An Introduction to Religious Experience and Behavior* (1958). All in all, however, during the twentieth century, modernism's affirmation of scientific truth resulted in religious dogma and religious institutions evoking suspicion and disregard rather than awe and admiration. Nevertheless, in spite of the significant decline of traditional religion in Western Europe and the outright persecution of religion in the Soviet Union, religion in much of the rest of the world has not only survived, but flourished.

In regard to counseling, although religious issues remained of concern throughout the century to such groups as the American Association of Pastoral Counselors, it took the American Psychological Association (APA) until the late 1970s to officially recognize religion as a legitimate area of interest and a possible influence on mental health. Behaviorism and environmental determinism had dominated counseling theory up to that time. Although the APA has published several volumes on religion and spirituality, much of modern psychology continues to focus on genetics, brain mechanisms, and biophysiology.

Postmodernism

Recent postmodernism began to flower among mid-twentieth-century, post–World War II culture in literature and philosophy, although it owed its beginning ancestry to the romantic reaction of literature in the early 1800s (in which scientific reductive explanations were accused of losing the essential beauty of nature). Three postmodern tenets are of particular importance to the assertion that Christian counseling can flourish in its environment. First is postmodernism's contention that there is a difference between words and truths. On the surface, this is simply an updating of the nominalist/realist debate and Immanuel Kant's claim that perception always mediates our observations, that is, we never see "the thing as such." Although a bit of an overstatement, it is often said that modernism contends that when science calls something by a name, there is a one-to-one relationship between that label and the reality it represents. Postmodernism asserts a name is a name—the word *represents* the reality. It is a word or label—nothing more (the nominalist point of view). As human beings we are forced to deal with *representations*—words that function to organize sensations and enhance communication but that remain words, not realities. In a sense, postmodernism takes an Aristotelian rather than a Platonic point of view. Words are not copies of reality; they are labels for reality.

Postmodernism contends, in the second place, that science is influenced by unexamined and implicit forces in the way it functions. The very labels as well as investigative processes of science are colored by *ideology*. Any claim of science that it merely describes reality is false. *Ideology* is the term for self-interest, bias, point of view, prejudgement. Postmodernism contends that much modernistic thinking is permeated and predetermined by unstated and implicit assumptions. Thomas Kuhn's *Structure of Scientific Revolutions* (1970) illustrates this contention. Kuhn contended that the history of science did not evidence a straight-line accumulation of objective empirical knowledge but rather a series of ideas surrounding hypothetical paradigms that guided research for a period of time but gave way to new paradigms over time. The model for understanding the development of science was more a series of circles than a straight line. Scientists did research within predetermined research paradigms (normal science) until there arose a revolution based on a new model, which, in turn, guided investigations only for a time. This revolutionary theory was grounded in a Hegelian thesis-antithesis-synthesis sequence that challenged the progressive, positivistic assumptions of modernism. Called *deconstructionism,* postmodernism has analyzed many conclusions for their patriarchal, imperialistic, and/or cultural bias.

Last, postmodernism asserts that because all ideas are riddled with ideologies, there are no absolutes, that is, everything is relative. There are no foundational truths that apply to all people, at all times, in all places. This does not mean that humans do not *act* as if their point of view is absolutely and basically true. They do. But it does mean that the proper stance toward ideas is one of confession and humility, that is, admitting that a given idea is true for *me* coupled with a tolerance of ideas that are true for *others*.

Postmodernism and Christian Counseling

It is our contention that these three postmodern assertions provide an environment supportive of Christian counseling. What might appear to some as postmodern problems for Christian counseling are actually augmentations and validations. In regard to the first observation that all knowledge is representational rather than empirically descriptive, Christian counseling is grounded in the *faith* that reality is not what it appears to be. The insight of faith as we have described it starts with the essential proclamation that God *is* and that God loves and cares for human beings. Although it may be uncomfortable to suggest that Christian counseling is basically a *naming* or *labeling* rather than an *absolutely valid description* of reality, it should be remembered that "faith" has always been understood to be qualitatively different from daily human reasoning. Hebrews' statement clearly affirms this point of view: "Faith is the assurance of things hoped for, the conviction of things not seen" (11:1).

Next, in regard to implicit ideology, Christian counseling is explicit and forthright. Postmodernism has sometimes been accused of being unable to affirm the truth-value of *any* statement because it presumes nothing is free of being filtered through some point of view. Christian counseling states its position up front and claims that its assumptions work for those who adopt its point of view. Christian counseling is impositional and persuasive. It makes no pretense of being otherwise. The "hermeneutic of suspicion" with which postmodernism questions most propositions is embraced by

Christian counseling. It is unapologetic about its ideology and agrees with postmodernism's concern about unadmitted presuppositions. Although to the eyes of faith Christian counseling proclaims that which is *absolutely true*, it recognizes that this is a *confessional* statement that functions to help people under success, under stress, and under distress (i.e., at all periods of life). It works for those who affirm its ideology!

Finally, Christian counseling admits it exists in a relativistic world. Postmodernism is absolutely correct in its assertion that no one point of view can automatically assert or prove its superiority to another point of view because *all* positions are grounded in a set of basic assumptions, that is, an ideology. This allows Christian counseling to claim a place at the table of counseling options without being discounted or disapproved. Any "political correctness" that would disallow Christian counseling a voice should be declared a hangover from modernism. As O'Donohue and Caselles (2005) noted, all theories of counseling should be judged on their effects in helping persons handle the crises of living rather than on the judgment that their concepts are true or not. Relativism is here to stay and Christian counseling should not be timid in asking to be heard.

In conclusion, although some would feel threatened by postmodernism, we contend that all concepts are terms applied to perceptions rather than exact descriptions of reality; that all concepts are riddled with ideologies; and that all theories are equally viable assumptions that provide support for Christian counseling. Christian counselors should boldly declare their assumptions and demonstrate the helpfulness of their approach. Relativity is not a threat to those who claim to have the word of life for a waiting world (cf. John 3:16).

Reference List

Anderson, R. S. 1990. *Christians who counsel.* Grand Rapids: Academic and Professional Books.

Augsburger, D. 1986. *Pastoral counseling across cultures.* Louisville: Westminster John Knox Press.

———. 1996. *Helping people forgive.* Louisville: Westminster John Knox Press.

Barth, K. 1956. *Christ and Adam.* Edinburgh: Oliver and Boyd.

Beit-Hallahmi, B. 1977. Psychology and religion 1880–1930: The rise and fall of a psychological movement. *Journal of the History of the Behavioral Sciences* 10:24-90.

———. 1986. Religion as art and identity. *Religion* 16:1-17.

Bowen, M. 1978. *Family theory in clinical practice.* New York: Jason Aronson.

Bragg, R. 1997. *All over but the shoutin'.* New York: Random House.

Browning, D. 1976. *The moral context of pastoral care.* Philadelphia: Westminster Press.

———. 1983. *Religious ethics and pastoral care.* Philadelphia: Fortress Press.

Browning, D. S., and T. D. Cooper. 2004. *Religious thought and the modern psychologies.* 2nd ed. Minneapolis: Fortress Press.

Byne, W., and B. Parsons. 1993. Human sexual orientation: The biological theories reappraised. *Archives of General Psychiatry* 50:222-39.

Cahoone, L., ed. 1996. *From modernism to postmodernism: An anthology.* Cambridge, MA: Blackwell.

Drane, J. 2004. Community, mystery, and the future of the church. In S. Holt and G. Preece, eds. *The bible and the business of life.* Adelaide: ATF Press.

Ellis, A. 1956. *The case against religion.* (audiotape) New York: Center for Rational-Emotive Psychotherapy.

Gilke, Langdon. *Maker of heaven and earth.* Garden City, NY: Doubleday, 1959.

Hart, P., and R. Osborne. 1988. *Concurrent counseling: An integrative approach to counseling by pastor and psychologist.* Pasadena, CA: Integration Press.

Hauerwas, S. 1975. *Character and the Christian life.* San Antonio: Trinity University Press.

Hays, R. 2003. The biblical witness concerning homosexuality. In M. D. Dunnam and H. N. Malony, eds. *Staying the course: Supporting the church's position on homosexuality,* 65-84. Nashville: Abingdon Press.

Reference List

Hoffman, J. 1979. *Ethical confrontation in counseling*. Chicago: University of Chicago Press.

Jones, L. 1995. *Embodying forgiveness*. Grand Rapids: Eerdmans.

Jones, S. L., and R. E. Butman. 1991. *Modern psychotherapies: A comprehensive Christian appraisal*. Downer's Grove, IL: InterVarsity Press.

Kellenberger, J. 1995. *Relationship morality*. University Park: Pennsylvania State University Press.

Kimper, F. 1972. Lecture notes. Claremont, CA: Claremont School of Theology. Unpublished.

Kraus, C. N. 1979. *The community of the spirit*. Grand Rapids: Eerdmans.

Kuhn, T. 1970. *The structure of scientific revolutions*. 2nd ed. Chicago: University of Chicago Press.

Laing, R. D. 1971. *The politics of the family*. New York: Pantheon Books.

Lehman, E. C. 1974. Academic discipline and faculty religiosity. *Journal for the Scientific Study of Religion* 13 (no. 2): 205-20.

Luckoff, D. and R. Turner and F. Lu. Psychoreligious dimensions of healing. *Journal of Transpersonal Psychology*, 24(1), 41-60.

MacIntyre, A. 1984. *After virtue*. Notre Dame, IN: Notre Dame University Press.

Malony, H. N. 1983. God talk in psychotherapy. In H. N. Malony, ed. *Wholeness and holiness: Readings in the psychology/theology of mental health*, 269-80. Grand Rapids: Baker.

———. 1989. *When getting along seems impossible*. Old Tappan, NJ: Revell.

———. 1995. *Integration musings: Thoughts on being a Christian professional*, rev. ed., Pasadena: Integration Press.

———. 1996. How counselors can help people become more spiritual through religious assessment. In H. Grzymala-Moszczyńska and B. Beit-Hallahmi, eds. *Religion, psychopathology and coping*, 245-62. Amsterdam: Rodolph.

———. 1998. Counseling body/soul persons. *International Journal for the Psychology of Religion* 8 (no. 4): 221-42.

———. 2001. Good, better, best: Dealing with religion in counseling. Address delivered at the meeting of the Christian Association of Psychological Studies, Western Region. April 16, 2002. San Diego, CA.

Mayers, M. K. 1978. The Filipino Samaritan: A parable of responsible cross-cultural behavior. *Missiology* 6 (no. 4): 463-66.

McClendon, J. 1986. *Ethics: systematic theology*. Vol. 1. Nashville: Abingdon Press.

McCullough, M., S. Sandage, and E. Worthington. 1997. *To forgive is human*. Downer's Grove, IL: InterVarsity Press.

Mueller-Fahrenholz, G. 1997. *Vergebung macht frei: Vorschlaege fuer eine theologie der versoehnung*. Frankfurt: Otto Lembeck.

Murphy, J., and J. Hampton. 1988. *Forgiveness and mercy*. Cambridge: Cambridge University Press.

Niebuhr, H. R. 1951. *Christ and culture*. New York: Harper.

Nouwen, H. 1992. *Life of the beloved: Spiritual living in a secular world*. New York: Crossroad.

Oden, T. C. 1966. *Kerygma and counseling: toward a covenant ontology for secular psychotherapy*. Philadelphia: Westminster Press.

O'Donohue, W. T., and C. E. Caselles. 2005. Homophobia: Conceptual, definitional, and value issues. In R. H. Wright and N. A. Cummings, eds. *Destructive trends in mental health: The well-intentional path to harm*. New York: Routledge.

Pattison, S. 1988. *A critique of pastoral care*. London: SCM Press.

Patton, J. 1990. *Is human forgiveness possible?* Nashville: Abingdon Press.

Phillips, D. L. 1987. Authenticity or morality? In R. Kruschwitz and R. Roberts, eds. *The virtues*. Belmont, CA: Wadsworth Publishing.

159

Reference List

Pruyser, P. W. 1976. *The minister as diagnostician: Personal problems in pastoral perspective.* Philadelphia: Westminster Press.

Rogers, C. R. 1957. The necessary and sufficient conditions of therapeutic personality change. *Journal of Consulting Psychology* 21:95-103.

Rooke-Ley, M. 2005. Laws force universities to discriminate. In the Eugene, OR, *Register-Guard.* December 4, 2005. Sec. B. Pages 1 and 4.

Sample, T., and A. E. DeLong. 2000. *The loyal opposition: Struggling with the church on homosexuality.* Nashville: Abingdon Press.

Schreurs, Agneta 2001. *Psychotherapy and Spirituality: Integating the Spiritual Dimension into Therapeutic Practice.* London: Jessica Kingsley Publishers.

Smedes, L. B. 2003. *My God and I: A spiritual memoir.* Grand Rapids: Eerdmans.

Sobrino, J. 1994. *The principle of mercy: Taking crucified people from the cross.* New York: Orbis.

Southard, S. 1989. *Theology and therapy: The wisdom of God in the context of friendship.* Dallas: Word.

Tan, S-Y. 1996. Religion in clinical practice: Implicit and explicit integration. In E. Shafranske, ed. *Religion and the clinical practice of psychology,* 365-87. Washington, DC: American Psychological Association.

Tillich, P. 1952. *The courage to be.* New Haven: Yale University Press.

———. 1954. *Love, power, and justice.* New York: Oxford University Press.

Truax, C., and R. Carkhuff. 1967. *Toward effective counseling and psychotherapy training and practice.* Chicago: Aldine.

Vitz, P. 1994. *Psychology as religion: The cult of self-worship.* 2nd ed. Grand Rapids: Eerdmans.

Winnicott, D. W. 1971. *Playing and reality.* New York: Basic Books.

Wogaman, J. P. 1989. *Christian moral judgment.* Louisville: Westminster John Knox Press.

Yevtushenko, Y. 1967. *Yevtushenko's reader.* New York: Avon.

Further Readings

Allport, Gordon W. *The Individual and His Religion: A Psychological Interpretation.* New York: Macmillan, 1950.

American Psychological Association Division 44/ Committee on Lesbian, Gay, and Bisexual Concerns Joint Task Force on Guidelines for Psychotherapy with Lesbian, Gay, and Bisexual Clients. "Guidelines for Psychotherapy with Lesbian, Gay, and Bisexual Clients." *American Psychologist* 55 (2000):1440-51.

Augsburger, David. *Dissident Discipleship.* Grand Rapids: Brazos Press, 2006.

———. *Hate-work: Working through the Pain and Pleasures of Hate.* Louisville: Westminster John Knox Press, 2004.

Clark, Walter H. *The Psychology of Religion: An Introduction to Religious Experience and Behavior.* New York: Macmillan, 1958.

Dunnam, Maxie D., and H. Newton Malony, eds. *Staying the Course: Supporting the Church's Position on Homosexuality.* Nashville: Abingdon Press, 2003.

Freud, Sigmund. *The Future of an Illusion.* New York: Doubleday, 1927.

Kerr, Michael, and Murray Bowen. *Family Evaluation: An Approach Based on Bowen Theory.* New York: W. W. Norton, 1988.

Kruschwitz, Robert B., and Robert C. Roberts. *The Virtues: Contemporary Essays on Moral Character.* Belmont, CA: Wadsworth, 1987.

Malony, H. Newton. "Assessing Religious Maturity." In *Psychotherapy and the Religiously Committed Patient,* edited by E. Mark Stern, 25-33. New York: Haworth Press, 1985.

———. "The Clinical Assessment of Optimal Religious Functioning." *Review of Religious Research* 30, no. 1 (1988): 3-17.

———, ed. *Current Perspectives in the Psychology of Religion.* Grand Rapids: Eerdmans, 1977.

———. "Pastoral Counseling and Sexual Identity." *Journal of Psychology and Christianity,* 2006. In press.

———. "The Uses of Religious Assessment in Counseling." In *Psychology of Religion,* edited by Laurence B. Brown, 3-18. London: SPCK, 1988.

Richards, P. Scott, and Allen E. Bergin, eds. *Handbook of Psychotherapy and Religious*

Further Readings

Diversity. Washington, DC: American Psychological Association, 2000.

———. *A Spiritual Strategy for Counseling and Psychotherapy.* Washington, DC: American Psychological Association, 1997.

Shafranske, Edward P., ed. *Religion and the Clinical Practice of Psychology.* Washington DC: American Psychological Association, 1996.

Tan, Siang-Yang. "Explicit Integration in Counseling." *Christian Journal of Psychology and Counseling 5*, no. 2 (1990): 7-13.

Wright, Rogers H., and Nicholas A. Cummings, eds. *Destructive Trends in Mental Health: The Well-intentioned Path to Harm.* New York: Routledge, 2005.

Index

Index

Index

MacIntyre, Alasdair, 79, 91
Malony, H. Newton, 5, 29, 39, 49, 105, 116, 137
mature Christians, 48
Mayers, Marvin, 120
McClendon, James, 90
McCullough, Michael, 55
mercy, 53, 59, 60-61
moral presuppositions, 84
moral reasoning, 87-89, 124
Mueller-Fahrenholz, G., 54
Murphy, Jeffrey, 61

Niebuhr, Reinhold, 38
Niebuhr, Richard, 133
Nouwen, Henri, 4, 5

O'Donohue, W. T., 157
Oglesby, William, 81
Osborne, Ralph, 41

pastoral care specialists, 71
pastoral counseling, 13
Pattison, Stephen, 89
Patton, John, 55
Phillips, D., 78
postmodernism, viii, 153-57
problems, definition of, 106
Pruyser, Paul W., vii, 45, 47

rational emotive therapy, 14
reconciler, 24
reconciliation, 67
reign of God, 125
religion, 29, 100
religious experience, 5
religious status inventory and interview, 45-49
reparative therapy, 131-32
Rogers, Carl, 4, 77

Sandage, Steven, 55
scholarly distance, 21
Schreurs, T. C., 62
scripture and text, 81-84, 126
self-esteem, 109

Sermon on the Mount, 52
sexual diversity, 130-35
sexual orientation, 133
Smedes, Lewis, 133
Sobrino, Jon, 61
Society for Christian Psychology, vi
South Africa, 50, 60, 62
spiritual directors, 71
spirituality, 5, 6, 28, 76
Stalin, Joseph, 52
supervision of counseling, 69
systems theory of family, 141

talking therapy, 19
theology defined, 126-27
theory development, 22-25
    facts, 22
    hypothetical constructs, 24
    intervening variables, 22, 25
    mediating constructs, 23
    proof, 23
therapeutic relationship, 71
Tillich, Paul, 60
Transactional Analysis, 12, 20
transempirical reality, 97
triangles and triangulation, 144, 147
Trinity, 95-97
Truax, C., and Carkhuff, R., 80
truth, 59-62, 79
    as an absolute, 5, 24
    kinds of, 62
Truth and Reconciliation Commission, 50, 60, 62
Turner, Robert, 45

unconditional positive regard, 4, 61, 81

value of life, 85
virtue and vision in ethics, 89-91, 126
Vitz, Paul, 20

Wesley, John, 112
westernization, 123
Winnicott, D. W., 28
Wogaman, J. Philip, 84
Worthington, Everett, 55